RAVES FOR *MARVIN'S ROOM*

"Deathly comedy and graveyard humor. . . . Death has rarely seemed so interesting or love so complex."
—CLIVE BARNES, *New York Post*

"The ultimate comedy for the '90s."   **—*USA Today***

"One of the funniest plays . . . as well as one of the wisest and most moving."   **—FRANK RICH, *New York Times***

"An unflinching yet surprisingly funny play about illness, physical and mental. . . . Playwright Scott McPherson has an original voice, balanced between sentiment and surrealism, and a gift for creating characters who are more than the sum of their behavior."   **—*Time***

"Beautifully written and deeply moving . . . breathtakingly combines the ridiculous and bizarre with the poignant and profound in an illuminating juxtaposition."
—*Chicago Tribune*

"It is McPherson's great and original gift to make his characters and their fates seem almost shamefully comical and honestly honest at every moment."   **—*Chicago Sun-Times***

SCOTT McPHERSON was an actor and writer. His first full-length play, *'Til the Fat Lady Sings*, was nominated for a Joseph Jefferson Citation for Best New Work. In addition to writing a one-act play, *Scraped*, he wrote television shows for Fox, WGN-TV, and NBC. He received the 1991 Whiting Writer's Award for *Marvin's Room*, and *Marvin's Room* won the 1992 New York Drama Desk Award for Best Play. Scott McPherson died in 1992.

SCOTT McPHERSON

MAR-VIN'S ROOM

Ⓟ

A PLUME BOOK

PLUME

Published by the Penguin Group
Penguin Books USA Inc., 375 Hudson Street,
New York, New York 10014, U.S.A.
Penguin Books Ltd, 27 Wrights Lane, London W8 5TZ, England
Penguin Books Australia Ltd, Ringwood, Victoria, Australia
Penguin Books Canada Ltd, 10 Alcorn Avenue,
Toronto, Ontario, Canada M4V 3B2
Penguin Books (N.Z.) Ltd, 182–190 Wairau Road, Auckland 10,
New Zealand

Penguin Books Ltd, Registered Offices:
Harmondsworth, Middlesex, England

First published by Plume, an imprint of Dutton Signet, a division
of Penguin Books USA Inc.

First Printing, September, 1992
7   9   10   8   6

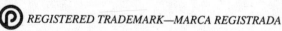 REGISTERED TRADEMARK—MARCA REGISTRADA

LIBRARY OF CONGRESS CATALOGING-IN-PUBLICATION DATA:
McPherson, Scott.
Marvin's room / Scott McPherson.
p.   cm.
ISBN 0-452-27819-8
I. Title.
PS3563.C394M37   1992
812'.54—dc20   92-53545
CIP

Printed in the United States of America
Set in Times Roman and Futura
Designed by Steven N. Stathakis

For Danny

INTRODUCTION
BY LARRY KRAMER

There are plays and there are playwrights; and there are the circumstances under which playwrights write their plays.

There are not so many plays like *Marvin's Room*.

There are not so many young playwrights like Scott McPherson, who has written facing the eminent possibility of his own death at any moment, while, at this same terrifying time, watching, waiting, and fearing the approaching death of the one he loves most.

So many of us enduring this awful plague of AIDS have either avoided writing anything about it, or have been unable to do so. This particular plague has prompted surprisingly little in the way of decent art created by those actually ill with the disease or those somehow touched by it, which should be just about everyone and anyone anywhere. I'm not certain why this is so, because other afflictions have produced their masterpieces. I suppose AIDS is presently more awful to bear in both life and art.

Scott McPherson has AIDS, as did his lover, Danny Sotomayor. When I started writing this introduction it was impossible to predict if both of them would be alive by the time this wonderful play of Scott's—in which he writes with all the lack of bathos I am having great difficulty circumventing here—reached print, and you'd be holding it in your hands.

This life of fragility is now forced on too many, particularly the young. Kids in their teens, young people in their twenties and thirties, all completely surrounded by death, wherever each looks, in every direction, the death of almost everyone and everything meaningful, the death of almost all one has hoped for and been prepared for and educated for and fought for. How do you find any meaning at all in life when all about you is destroyed? Where do you find hope? How? Where do you find God? How do you go on? How do you prepare yourself? For the end of life. So *soon*.

And how do you create?

Scott and Danny shared the same hospital room. They lay in beds next to each other, staring into each other's eyes, wordlessly. Scott was terrified Danny was going to die. Danny couldn't speak anymore, because lesions had destroyed his lungs. And he was terrified to go to sleep, for fear he wouldn't wake up.

Danny died at seven in the morning on February 5, 1992. The disease had spread to every part of his body. Finally his heart just stopped. He was thirty-three years old.

Marvin's Room is not a play about AIDS. And *Marvin's Room* is not a gay play. Yet *Marvin's Room* is a magnificent gay play about AIDS.

And my desire to introduce this magnificent achievement has less to do with honoring it as something important written by a gay writer and more to do with acknowledging the inestimable courage of that gay writer. Scott McPherson has had the guts to write in the face of the most awful circumstances imaginable—the fates and the furies, pitilessly, hurling garbage at him and his life and his world, nonstop.

"I'm afraid to close my eyes. I'll close my eyes and I won't wake up," Bessie says in *Marvin's Room*.

"I'm trying to be brave. But I'm scared. I'm so scared." Bessie says this, too.

Two lovers slowly dying side by side in their shared hospital room is the most awful of images. Shivering under adjoining blankets. Scott unable to keep food down and uncontrollably vomiting and shitting, sometimes in the middle of the floor before a toilet or a bedpan can be reached. Danny's lungs bleeding and his oxygen intake dropping.

I can't erase that image since hearing about it. It's fearful to visualize and fearful to contemplate. No one should have to live and die like this. And yet so many of us do. More and more of us.

Danny had managed to get to New York for the opening of Scott's play. Danny was hugely proud of Scott, proud not only of their love but of their creative partnership—two artists (Danny was a brilliant political cartoonist), not only in love with each other but admiring and respectful of each other's work, accomplishments, and goals. There is a line in one of my own plays, *The Normal Heart*, in which Felix, the lover who will die of AIDS, tells Ned, the man he will fall in love with, "You know, my fantasy has always been to go away and live by the ocean and write twenty-four novels, living with someone just like you with all these books who of course will be right there beside me, writing your own twenty-four novels." Scott and Danny had that infinitely rare and loving creative partnership. Two artists, in love with each other, supporting each other in their hearts and their art. I don't know of any artist who doesn't want this kind of love.

The last time I saw Scott and Danny together was a few days after opening night, a few days after Frank Rich's extraordinary rave review in the *New York Times* made *Marvin's Room* the hit it deserves to be, assuring it many future productions around the world. A playwright's dream come true! I visited with them in a rather tacky suite in some hotel I'd never heard of way up West End Avenue. Danny looked wretched. He had little hair left because the chemotherapy for his pulmonary Kaposi's sarcoma had taken it away. His voice was a harsh whisper, painful for him to emit. He could hardly talk, but he was so happy and proud of Scott's success. "Did you see that review?" he asked me over and over.

Scott had barely got out of the hospital in time to make it to his own opening. He'd come down, again, with one of the many horrible "opportunistic infections" those with AIDS come down with, again and again, and spend their time trying to get over, throw off, so they might have a little bit more time left fighting to live just a little bit longer, a few more days, a few more minutes. He hadn't even been able to come to the New York rehearsals.

It's impossible to get out of my mind all the ironies and sadnesses and pleasures of that visit, all mixed up for them and for me as well. Here were these two young men, half-dead, sitting side by side, each valiantly and lovingly trying to keep the other alive—Danny trying to make Scott swallow some soup and Scott trying to get Danny to eat a bit of soggy tuna-fish sandwich between his wracking coughs.

And there I sit, trying to get them both to concentrate on more mundane matters. Neither knows anything about agents and lawyers and representation. "Scott, we must get your play published. Danny, you must get me xeroxes of *all* your cartoons, so we can work on the book you want. Both of you, you must call all these people who might be interested. I've written their names and phone numbers on this napkin. Do you have a lawyer? Either of you? Do you have a will? Both of you? What instructions do you want followed regarding your work? . . ." (I have been through this enough times not to be shy about getting to the point.)

And each looks at me as if he understands, and each nods as if he will make all the calls the very moment he's back home in Chicago.

Scott, still very weak, has the euphoria of Frank Rich's review to buoy him.

But, as Danny spits up his tuna-fish sandwich, the glory of a *New York Times* review is suddenly far away.

And returning to Chicago, Scott has a relapse and Danny weakens considerably and they both wind up in those twin hospital beds.

How does anyone go on?

"I've had such love in my life. I look back and I've had such love," Bessie says, answering this cosmic question. "I am so lucky to have been able to love someone so much," she says again, only seconds later.

Scott told me that he wrote this play before he'd met Danny and before he himself got really sick. "All I was was only HIV positive. All that happened is my life caught up to the play."

But between these "all"s is everything. In each "all" are too many years of a plague, and of—if not yet dying from it oneself—watching the dying. These "all"s embrace this artist, giving sights and sounds to the witnessed suffering, which is taken in, to be used . . . whenever.

I hope that somehow I've been able to convey the circumstances and context of this remarkable play: how life *can* forge art, hacking it out of a few breaths—be they Bessie's or Danny's—grabbed and greedily gulped here and there, and a few bits of food that stay down, and a few peaceful moments of love when you don't have to vomit or shit or take your medicine. And all this while trying, against all odds, and lest it destroy *all* hope, to ignore a largely uncaring world.

Now Scott is living through that wretched host of bodily agonies that destroyed his lover. He is enduring them as bravely as Danny did. He still thinks of *Marvin's Room* as a hopeful play, "without turning a blind-eye from the horrors, of course."

Once again I wonder how he, how any of us, still finds hope.

Ah well, I hope that when I die I can accept the fact, as Scott has accepted it and as Danny did as well, that we did the best we could. That—somehow—we lived, for a while, through these awful years of plague. And created. And bore witness.

And, yes, with hope.

New York City
May 1992

Marvin's Room premiered on February 19, 1990, at the Goodman Theatre Studio in Chicago, with the following cast:

BESSIE	Laura Esterman
DR. WALLY	Tim Monsion
RUTH	Jane MacIver
BOB	Peter Rybolt
LEE	Lee Guthrie
DR. CHARLOTTE	Ora Jones
HANK	Mark Rosenthal
EXPECTANT FATHER	Peter Rybolt
CHARLIE	Karl Maschek
RETIREMENT HOME DIRECTOR	Ora Jones
MARVIN	William T. Gallagher

Director:	David Petrarca
Set design:	Linda Buchanan
Costume design:	Claudia Boddy
Lighting design:	Robert Christen
Music composition and sound design:	Rob Milburn
Production stage manager:	Kimberly Osgood
Dramaturgs:	Tom Creamer and Sandy Shinner

Marvin's Room opened on November 16, 1990, at the Hartford Stage Company in Hartford, Connecticut, with the following cast:

BESSIE	Laura Esterman
DR. WALLY	Tim Monsion
RUTH	Marylouise Burke
BOB	Peter J. Ludwig
LEE	Janet Zarish
DR. CHARLOTTE	Aleta Mitchell
HANK	Mark Rosenthal
CHARLIE	Karl Maschek
RETIREMENT HOME DIRECTOR	Aleta Mitchell
MARVIN	Gerald Forbes

Director:	David Petrarca
Set design:	Linda Buchanan
Costume design:	Claudia Boddy
Lighting design:	Robert Christen
Music composition and sound design:	Rob Milburn
Production stage manager:	Barbara Reo
Casting:	Julie Mossberg and Brian Chavanne
Dramaturg:	Greg Leaming

Marvin's Room opened on December 5, 1991, at Playwrights Horizons in New York City, with the following cast:

BESSIE	Laura Esterman
DR. WALLY	Tim Monsion
RUTH	Alice Drummond
BOB	Tom Aulino
LEE	Lisa Emery
DR. CHARLOTTE	Shona Tucker
HANK	Mark Rosenthal
CHARLIE	Karl Maschek
RETIREMENT HOME DIRECTOR	Shona Tucker
MARVIN	Adam Chapnick

Director:	David Petrarca
Set design:	Linda Buchanan
Costume design:	Claudia Boddy
Lighting design:	Robert Christen
Music composition and sound design:	Rob Milburn
Production stage manager:	Roy Harris
Casting:	Daniel Swee
Production manager:	David A. Milligan

CHARACTERS
(IN ORDER OF APPEARANCE)

BESSIE
DR. WALLY
RUTH
BOB
LEE
DR. CHARLOTTE
HANK
CHARLIE
RETIREMENT HOME DIRECTOR
MARVIN

TIME

The present.

PLACE

Various locations in Florida and a mental institution in
Ohio.

PLAYWRIGHT'S NOTE

My grandmother was the first "dying" person I ever knew. I already knew a dead person: my father. Dad, who was once a race car driver and then a married Volkswagen salesman with three baby boys, drove the baby-sitter home and on his way back to us wrapped his car around a telephone pole, killing himself and disrupting phone conversations on the east side of Columbus for a good couple of hours. But I never thought of my father as a "dying" person. He was alive—and then simply dead.

It was my grandmother who was "dying," her cancer-ridden body resting in the upstairs bedroom where the only TV in the house stood at the foot of her bed. If you wanted to watch "Ed Sullivan," and I did, you also had to watch grandmother, commercials and morphine injections coming at regular intervals. It was a situation that, to a child, seemed neither odd nor morbid.

My mother was to be grandmother's chief caregiver, raise three children, keep house, and work part-time as a sales clerk at Lazarus department store. My mother, who studied modern dance in college and married a race car driver against her parents' wishes, threw herself at her responsibilities with a terrifying determination—afraid if she gave any less she would awaken to find she was running off in the other direction, leaving all of us behind to fend for ourselves.

Now I am thirty-one and my lover has AIDS. Our friends have AIDS. And we all take care of each other, the less sick caring for the more sick. At times, an unbelievably harsh fate is transcended by a simple act of love, by caring for another.

By most, we are thought of as "dying." But as dying becomes a way of life, the meaning of the word blurs.

Chicago
January 1992

ACT ONE
SCENE ONE

(A doctor's examining room. BESSIE, a woman of forty years, sits. A DOCTOR is seated next to her. He holds a syringe.)

BESSIE: I suppose I should tell you needles bother me a little.

DR. WALLY: Oh *(he shudders)*, I know what you mean. All right, Augustina, could you give me your arm please? Do you mind if I call you Augustina?

BESSIE: Well, my name is Bessie.

DR. WALLY: Bessie. Of course. I'm sorry. Things have been a bit hectic around here. Dr. Serat is away on vacation, and this morning our receptionist quit. Usually Nurse Abrams would draw the blood for any blood tests but . . . where'd I put the whatchamacallit? The . . . uh . . . do you see it?

BESSIE: What?

DR. WALLY: You know, that . . . um . . . um . . . I tie it around your arm to make your veins pop out.

BESSIE: Tourniquet?

DR. WALLY: Yes, that's it. Oh, I'm sitting on it. How'd that happen? Okay, give me your arm, please.

BESSIE: Janine quit?

DR. WALLY: Uh-huh. Did you know her?

BESSIE: Only from here. I bring my father, Marvin, and my Aunt Ruth in quite a bit to see Dr. Serat. Why did she quit? Is she getting married?

DR. WALLY: No, no. Unbeknownst to any of us she was harboring a deep-seated phobia about cockroaches. She said she just couldn't work here any longer. It made her itch.

BESSIE (*looking around*): Oh?

DR. WALLY: I think I have seen you out front. Is your father fairly thin?

BESSIE: Dad's a bone. You could snap him like a twig.

DR. WALLY: He's somewhat pale?

BESSIE: He's as white as a bedsheet unless he's choking. Then he gets a little color.

DR. WALLY: He has trouble breathing?

BESSIE: No. He likes to put things in his mouth. I'll walk into his bedroom and he'll be lying there all blue in the face with the Yahtzee dice stuck down his throat. Do you know that game?

DR. WALLY: Yes.

BESSIE: It's a fun game, isn't it?

DR. WALLY: Yes.

BESSIE: Except Dad sucked all the ink off the dice, so it's hard to tell what you're rolling.

DR. WALLY: And your aunt—now this is odd, but I remember she kept staring at my shoes.

BESSIE: Ruth has three collapsed vertebrae in her back.

DR. WALLY: Oh, I'm sorry.

BESSIE: I'm always lugging one of them in here for something or other.

DR. WALLY: I hope they are both all right for the moment.

BESSIE: Oh, they're fine. Dad's dying, but he's been dying for about twenty years. He's doing it real slow so I don't miss anything. And Dr. Serat has worked a miracle with Ruth. She's had constant pain from her back since she was born, and now the doctor had her get an electronic anesthetizer—you know, they put the wires right into the brain, and when she has a bad pain she just turns her dial. It really is a miracle.

DR. WALLY: That's wonderful.

BESSIE: If she uses it in the kitchen our automatic garage door goes up. But that's a small price to pay, don't you think?

DR. WALLY *(he begins to tie the tourniquet on her arm):* It's amazing what they can do.

BESSIE: When does Dr. Serat get back from his trip?

DR. WALLY: Not till the end of the month. I'll have to hire a new receptionist without him.

BESSIE: What will you do about the bugs?

DR. WALLY: Bugs? Oh no, we don't have any bugs. That's the thing. It must have all been in her mind. She saw bugs everywhere. Granted, there are bugs everywhere in Florida, but none in these offices. *(He sets up some vials.)*

BESSIE: Are those all for me?

DR. WALLY: These here, I have a few in my pocket, and I'll have to scrape up a couple more out of one of these drawers.

BESSIE: That seems like a lot of blood.

DR. WALLY: Well, June, if it seems like a lot of blood, that's because it is. So if you're feeling anxious because we're drawing a lot of blood, you should. So what you're feeling is perfectly normal.

BESSIE: Bessie.

DR. WALLY: I'm sorry?

BESSIE: My name is Bessie.

DR. WALLY: Did I call you Augustina?

BESSIE: You called me June.

DR. WALLY: I did?

BESSIE: You're confusing me with your other patients.

DR. WALLY: No I'm not.

BESSIE: You called me June.

DR. WALLY: June is the name of my dog. So why don't we get this over with. Where are the . . . um . . . the . . . uh . . .

BESSIE: What?

DR. WALLY *(pulling out a bag of cotton balls)*: Here they are. The bag is sealed so they're still sterile. *(He opens the bag with his teeth.)*

BESSIE: How many days are left in this month? Maybe I should wait.

DR. WALLY: Well, let me find my . . . um . . . my . . . um . . . date thing.

BESSIE: Calendar?

DR. WALLY: Twenty-eight days.

BESSIE: I think I'll wait. It's just a vitamin deficiency, right?

DR. WALLY: I said it *might* be a vitamin deficiency. That is one, and the most probable, explanation for your fatigue and easy bruising. But we must rule out the other possibilities or we're not doing our job. And I wouldn't want Dr. Serat to think I'm neglecting his patients while he's away. Now this will only take a second.

BESSIE *(extending her arm;* DR. WALLY *positions the needle)*: I might pass out.

DR. WALLY: Would you rather lie down?

BESSIE: No. Now that I said it out loud I should be fine. I give Dad shots all the time. *(She pulls away again.)*

DR. WALLY: You know, when I was young and my doctor had to give me an ouch of some sort, he would tell me to look at the pattern on the linoleum floor, squint my eyes, and tell him what pictures I could make out of it. The ouch was over before I knew it.

BESSIE: That's real cute.

DR. WALLY: Why don't you try it?

BESSIE: I don't have your imagination.

DR. WALLY *(reaching behind her to get the needle from the cart):* Just look at the floor and tell me what you see.

(BESSIE *sees what he is up to and he turns her head back out front.)*

Just look at the floor and tell me what you see.

BESSIE: I see a big fat cockroach.

DR. WALLY: Where?

BESSIE: There.

(DR. WALLY *tries to step on it, misses, tries again, grabs a magazine and hits it under the cart.)*

DR. WALLY: That wasn't a cockroach.

BESSIE: What was it?

DR. WALLY: From the way it burst, I'd say some sort of bloodsucker.

BESSIE: I think I would like to lie down.

DR. WALLY: I'll see if the room is free.

(He exits.)

(BESSIE sits alone for a moment. She then raises her skirt to examine a deep bruise on her thigh.)

DR. WALLY *(entering):* Nurse Abrams is still in there with a patient.

BESSIE: Let's just get it over with.

NURSE'S VOICE *(offstage):* Doctor?!

DR. WALLY: Excuse me. Would you like a magazine?

(He offers her the magazine that he killed the bug with.)

BESSIE: I'm fine.

(DR. WALLY exits, then re-enters after a moment.)

DR. WALLY: Well . . . *(Pause.)* The room is free now.
BESSIE: That's all right. I'll sit.

(Blackout.)

SCENE TWO

(*Bessie's home.* MARVIN *lies in a bed behind the upstage wall, barely visible through glass bricks.* RUTH, *a woman of seventy years with a slight hunchback, sleeps in a chair.* BESSIE *enters with groceries. Her arms are bruised from the doctor's attempts to draw blood.*)

BESSIE: Aunt Ruth? Ruth?

RUTH: Hmmmmm.

BESSIE: Ruth, you're not supposed to sleep sitting in a chair, honey. It puts too much pressure on your lower spine.

RUTH: You're home.

BESSIE: Do you want to go lie down?

RUTH: Don't you look pretty.

BESSIE: Do you want to lie down?

RUTH: No, no. Don't you bother about me, now. I'm just fine.

BESSIE: You're sleeping in the chair.

RUTH: I am?

BESSIE: You were, when I came in. That's not good for you.

RUTH: Oh, stupid me. You tell me right away when I'm sleeping because I don't always know.

BESSIE: I just got home. I couldn't tell you sooner.

RUTH: Look, this control box pulled my sweater. I'm going to have a hole there. It's my own fault.

BESSIE: How's Dad?

RUTH: What did the doctor say?

BESSIE: Oh, he made a big to-do so I wouldn't feel like he was overcharging me.

RUTH: He's a nice man, isn't he. He has very handsome hands.

BESSIE: It wasn't Dr. Serat.

RUTH: Bessie, oh, what happened to your arms?

BESSIE: They took a little blood.

RUTH: It looks tender. Should you see a doctor?

BESSIE: I just came from the doctor.

RUTH: Did you show him your arms?

BESSIE: Yes, he just had some trouble finding my veins.

RUTH: That sounds serious.

BESSIE: I have a vitamin deficiency, Ruth, that's all.

RUTH: It's because you don't make stinky often enough.

BESSIE: I do so.

RUTH: Stinky is poison. You have to get rid of it. That's why when you're constipated you have a headache.

BESSIE (picking up Marvin's pills): Did you give Dad his five o'clock?

RUTH: What did I do? What time is it now?

BESSIE: Five twenty-five.

RUTH: No, but I was going to.

BESSIE: Honey, I asked you to do one thing.

RUTH: I'm so stupid. I'm useless, I know.

BESSIE: You are not.

RUTH: It's my cure, I think. It's because I have these wires in my brain.

BESSIE: It's not your cure. You blame your cure for everything.

RUTH: I can feel them. They tingle when I bathe.

BESSIE: You used to blame your pain, now you blame your cure.

RUTH: It's gotten so I'm afraid to get in the tub.

BESSIE: You've always been afraid to get in the tub.

RUTH: Oh, no, no, no. I've never been afraid to get in the tub.

BESSIE: You make me come in and towel down the floor.

RUTH: That's because I'm afraid to get *out* of the tub. The floor gets so wet. Do you remember Mrs. Steingetz fell and the poor thing cracked her head wide open? No one found her until her family came down for Thanksgiving, and even then not until the end of their visit.

BESSIE: I remember.

RUTH: She'd still be there if they hadn't run out of towels in the guest bath.

BESSIE: I know.

RUTH: I don't want to be lying on the tiles till the holiday season.

BESSIE: You won't.

RUTH: I mean, my goodness, it's only just June.

BESSIE: I hope you remembered to give Dad his four o'clock.

RUTH: Oh, stupid me.

BESSIE: Ruth, he is supposed to get his pills at the same time every day.

RUTH: I know, but—

BESSIE: You never forget to watch your program, do you? You never forget what time your show comes on.

RUTH: You usually give Marvin his pills.

BESSIE: Today I asked you to.

(BESSIE goes into Marvin's room to give him his pills while RUTH crosses to the kitchen to get her vitamins.)

I have been running all over today. Would you quit hogging the bed so I can sit down! Here. Take these now. We're a little off schedule today. . . . Have you been pulling at your sheets? You've got them all twisted. That can't be very comfortable. . . . What does that face mean? Mr. Innocent! . . . How about some tomato soup? And some juice? . . . Water? . . . Juice? . . . Which? . . . Juice.

(She re-enters.)

He's confused. He doesn't know why he's getting his four o'clock at five-thirty.

RUTH *(with her pills)*: Do you want to take one of mine for your deficiency?

BESSIE: I'll get some real vitamins later.

RUTH: These are real. They're just easier to swallow because I don't like to swallow things. Do you want Pebbles or Bam-Bam?

BESSIE: Ruth.

RUTH: Dino came out.

BESSIE: Dino's fine.

RUTH: Chew it up good. We have to take care of you, too. *(Slight pause.)* That cat came around today.

BESSIE: Honey, it's just a little kitty. It won't bother you.

RUTH: It came right up to the house and stared in at me. It sat there like it was stone.

BESSIE: Uh-huh.

RUTH: What do you think it wants?

BESSIE: I don't think it wants anything.

RUTH: I know you have things you have to do and it's hard getting someone to come in, but I wish you wouldn't leave me at home alone.

BESSIE: Honey, you do fine.

RUTH: But I'm so useless. What if Marvin were to choke on something again? What if he gets hold of the Yahtzee dice or tries to kill himself with the Parcheesi men?

BESSIE: Dr. Serat explained this to you. He puts things in his mouth because it gives him pleasure. He likes the way it feels. You know how much he likes it when you bounce the light off your compact mirror? This is another thing he likes. He's not trying to choke himself.

RUTH: What if he dies while you're out of the house?

BESSIE: Then you'll call me and I'll come home. *(Pause.)* You've got your cure now. There's no reason you can't help out around here. I don't ask you to do much.

RUTH: Do you want me to make the tomato soup?

BESSIE: No. You'd make a mess of it. *(She starts to make the soup.)*

RUTH: I'll go bounce the light around Marvin's room.

BESSIE: That's a good idea. Why don't you do that. And later we'll watch some TV. All right?

RUTH: All right.

(She goes into Marvin's room.)

BESSIE *(pouring a can of soup into a metal pan)*: Do you remember all the foods Dad used to like—flapjacks and bacon and eggs—

(RUTH moves her mirror above Marvin's bed.)

—and grits and biscuits and roast beef and green beans and mashed potatoes and apple pie and ice cream he churned himself.

(Lights fade to black. The bouncing light in Marvin's room is the last to go out.)

SCENE THREE

(The doctor's office. BESSIE sits alone. DR. WALLY enters with a bicycle wheel.)

DR. WALLY: I'm sorry to have kept you waiting—

BESSIE: You must be very busy.

DR. WALLY: —but I couldn't find a place to lock my bike.

BESSIE: Oh.

DR. WALLY: Well, how are we today?

BESSIE: You tell me.

DR. WALLY: That's a pretty dress you're wearing. Is it new?

BESSIE: It's the same one I always wear into town.

DR. WALLY: Well, I can see why.

BESSIE: I suppose it can't be good news or you would have just told me over the phone.

DR. WALLY: Your . . . um . . . Your . . . um . . .

BESSIE: Blood test.

DR. WALLY: It's our policy not to give any test results over the phone.

BESSIE: Oh. Because I really got myself worked up. I was thinking all sorts of horrible thoughts.

DR. WALLY: I certainly didn't mean to worry you. But I did think it would be a good idea for me to see you again.

BESSIE: Oh?

(The phone rings. DR. WALLY answers.)

DR. WALLY: Dr. Wally speaking. . . . Yes, I know I have someone waiting in my office. I am in my office. . . . That's all right. *(He hangs up.)*

BESSIE: Is there a problem?

DR. WALLY: No. He's just new. He'll get the hang of it.

BESSIE: I meant with my blood test. Did it get lost or something?

DR. WALLY: No, no. It didn't get lost. But I would like to run some other tests.

BESSIE: Oh, you would?

DR. WALLY: Simply to rule out certain possibilities.

BESSIE: Uh-huh.

DR. WALLY: We could take the sample now if you have the time.

BESSIE: What are the possibilities?

DR. WALLY: There are a number of possibilities I would like to rule out.

BESSIE: Are you still thinking I have a vitamin deficiency?

DR. WALLY: I think we may have ruled out that possibility.

BESSIE: Do you think we should? Should we rule that out?

DR. WALLY: Why don't we take this sample and then we'll have a better idea of what we're talking about.

(Pause.)

BESSIE: I left Aunt Ruth in charge of Dad. I shouldn't be gone long.

DR. WALLY: This won't take long.

(Pause. BESSIE *extends her arm.)*

DR. WALLY: That won't be necessary.

BESSIE: Oh. I think I'm too nervous to pee into a cup.

DR. WALLY: There's no reason to be nervous. What I am going to do is this: I am going to give you a local anesthetic and then I'm going to remove a little bone marrow from your hip.

BESSIE: What?

DR. WALLY: You won't really feel it. Maybe a slight pinching. Now, it will make a little noise so don't let that bother you.

BESSIE: You're going to take bone marrow out of my hip?

DR. WALLY: Just a little. There will be a crunching noise. If you've ever had your wisdom teeth pulled you know the sound. And you also know that it sounds worse than it is.

BESSIE: I've never had my wisdom teeth out.

DR. WALLY: Really. Hmmmm. Maybe you should see someone.

BESSIE: I've never had a problem with them.

DR. WALLY: Good teeth are a blessing. I've never had a cavity in my life.

BESSIE: I've had my share, I guess.

DR. WALLY: I'm no dentist, but as you get older, cavities aren't so much the problem. It's gum disease.

BESSIE: I always massage my gums and I brush my tongue.

DR. WALLY: Do you floss?

BESSIE: Not as often as I should.

DR. WALLY: Who does? Could you hike up your dress, please?

BESSIE: I don't mean to be nosy, but could you tell me why you're going to take bone marrow out of my hip?

DR. WALLY: There's not a lot of flesh on the hip.

BESSIE: But what is the test for?

DR. WALLY: Why don't you let me do the worrying for now?

BESSIE: I am probably thinking it's something much worse than it actually is.

DR. WALLY: I wouldn't waste your time thinking anything until we get the test results back.

BESSIE: Is it serious—like a brain tumor?

DR. WALLY: No, no.

BESSIE: M.S.?

DR. WALLY: No.

BESSIE: Cancer?

(Pause.)

Cancer?

DR. WALLY *(picks up the phone)*: Hold my calls, please. *(He hangs up.)* Bessie—

(The phone rings. He answers.)

Dr. Wally speaking. . . . Yes, that was me just then. Didn't you recognize my voice? . . . You can tell by which little light blinks on your phone. . . . That's all right. *(He hangs up.)* That's what I get for hiring my own brother. Bessie, first I should explain your blood test.

BESSIE: Okay.

DR. WALLY: You have something on your shoulder.

BESSIE: I do?

DR. WALLY: It's a button.

BESSIE: Is that bad?

DR. WALLY: No, it's part of your dress. I thought it was a bug. Believe it or not, we are having something of a problem with them after all. I'm not doing this very well.

BESSIE: Should I be worried?

DR. WALLY: No. Would you like a cup of coffee?

BESSIE: I'd love one.

DR. WALLY *(picks up his phone)*: This is Dr. Wally speaking. Please bring a cup of coffee to my office. *(He hangs up.)*

BESSIE: Could it have to do with whether or not I poo regularly?

DR. WALLY: We'll want to look at everything. But your blood work shows abnormally low levels of red cells, platelets, and mature white cells.

BESSIE: I haven't felt as bad lately. I haven't been nearly as tired.

DR. WALLY: That's good. Now, your spleen and your liver, on your last visit, felt slightly enlarged.

BESSIE: Is that bad?

DR. WALLY: Well, one of the possibilities that I am hoping to rule out is leukemia.

(Pause.)

BESSIE: Uh-huh.

(The phone rings.)

DR. WALLY: I don't have to answer it.

BESSIE: Pick it up.

DR. WALLY *(answering the phone)*: This is Dr. Wally speaking. . . .

(He cups the receiver and speaks to BESSIE.)

Do you take cream?

BESSIE: Yes.

DR. WALLY: Yes. And don't call me anymore, Bob. I mean it. *(He hangs up.)*

BESSIE: Odds are it's leukemia, right?

DR. WALLY: Odds don't mean anything. I could tell you that, yes, with your symptoms and your blood work the odds favor leukemia, but that doesn't mean anything. You're an individual, not a statistic.

BESSIE: But they do?

DR. WALLY: This is why I was reluctant to . . . You are worried now and you may not have cause to be.

BESSIE: What does it mean if it *is* leukemia?

DR. WALLY: What do you mean?

BESSIE: Is it still fatal?

DR. WALLY: What do you mean?

BESSIE: I mean, does it still kill you?

DR. WALLY: You must remember there are a variety of leukemias and a variety of treatments. Radiation therapy, chemotherapy. Bone marrow transplants, which a few years ago were considered experimental, are now a very real option. You do have family?

BESSIE: Dad and Ruth.

DR. WALLY: No other?

BESSIE: No.

DR. WALLY: Are you sure?

BESSIE: Yes.

DR. WALLY: I thought your file mentioned a sister.

BESSIE: Oh. Yes. I have a sister. Lee. Yes.

DR. WALLY: Well, we're getting a little ahead of ourselves anyway. No one said you had leukemia, so it's premature to talk of treatment options.

BESSIE: So you think I'm overreacting?

DR. WALLY: I understand your reaction.

BESSIE: My mother had leukemia.

DR. WALLY: I know.

BESSIE: You know?

DR. WALLY: Why don't we take this sample and you can get home to your father and your aunt.
BESSIE: All right.

(BOB enters.)

BOB: Coffee?
BESSIE: Oh, thank you.

(She takes the coffee. BOB exits. DR. WALLY raises her dress. BESSIE doesn't know what to do with the coffee.)

DR. WALLY: You can drink your coffee.

(BESSIE, standing, rapidly sips the too-hot coffee from the white styrofoam cup. DR. WALLY stands waiting, needle in hand. The lights fade to black as BESSIE repeatedly sips.)

SCENE FOUR

(*An institutional visiting room. There are three chairs. A* DOCTOR *sits in one.* LEE, *a woman in her late thirties, sits in another.*)

LEE: Do you mind if I smoke?

DR. CHARLOTTE: Yes. Thank you for asking.

LEE: How 'bout I blow it this way?

DR. CHARLOTTE: I'm afraid there's no smoking anywhere on this floor.

LEE: I'll be very quiet then. (*She lights up. Pause. She looks at her watch.*) I should have called, right?

DR. CHARLOTTE: They're getting him. He's in occupational therapy, which is in another building on the grounds.

LEE: Oh, I see.

DR. CHARLOTTE: It's good to see you here, Lee. May I call you Lee?

LEE: Sure.

DR. CHARLOTTE: We've missed you on other days. So has Hank.

LEE: I know. I wish I could visit more, but . . . well . . . you know.

DR. CHARLOTTE: Mm-hmm.

LEE: Now, you're not an orderly are you?

DR. CHARLOTTE: I'm a psychiatrist.

LEE: Are you who Hank talks to?

DR. CHARLOTTE: I'm in charge of his therapy. He talks to me and others on staff.

LEE: Well, you know he lies. I'm just telling you that—I mean, not because I think he's been saying bad things about me, but I'm sure he has been—I mean, I'm sure he has been—but you should know he lies to help you with his therapy.

DR. CHARLOTTE: Mm-hmm.

LEE: For instance, he told his guidance counselor at school that I beat him.

DR. CHARLOTTE: Mm-hmm.

LEE: So you see what I mean.

DR. CHARLOTTE: Mm-hmm.

LEE: Oh, see now, you're thinking, "Oh, I wonder if she *does* beat him."

DR. CHARLOTTE: Is that what you think I think?

LEE: Don't you?

DR. CHARLOTTE: Do you want me to think that?

LEE: What do you mean?

DR. CHARLOTTE: What do you think I mean?

LEE: What do you mean, "What do I think you mean?"?

DR. CHARLOTTE: What do you think I mean by "What do you think I mean?"?

(Pause.)

LEE: You wouldn't have an ashtray, would you?

(DR. CHARLOTTE takes a glass ashtray out and crosses to LEE.)

LEE: Do you want a drag?

(Pause.)

DR. CHARLOTTE: No. Here. *(She hands the ashtray to LEE.)* We'd like to have you become more involved in Hank's therapy. We'd like you to come more often for visits.

LEE: Doctor, can I be honest with you? What is your first name?

DR. CHARLOTTE: Charlotte.

LEE: Oh, my youngest boy's a Charlie.

DR. CHARLOTTE: Yes.

LEE: Charlotte. I've forced myself through school and I'm about to get my degree. I'm very picky now about the kind of man I'll go with. I keep—I used to keep a very clean house. Hank makes fun of my degree in cosmetology. He terrorizes any man I'm interested in. This last one, Lawrence, Hank made fun of his being on parole, made fun of the way he held his liquor, made fun of his Pinto. The point is, Hank cost me a potentially good relationship. And as for my house . . . Hank is not something I can control, so what is the point of my visiting?

DR. CHARLOTTE: He says he misses you.

(HANK enters. He is a big seventeen-year-old covered with motor grease.)

LEE: Look at you. You look like a pig.

HANK: I'm working on an engine.

LEE: Don't they let you shower?

HANK: They told me you were here and I was supposed to come here.

LEE: Don't sit down, Hank.

(He sits.)

You'll get the chair all greasy. *(Slight pause.)* Are you behaving yourself?

HANK: They're not strapping me down anymore.

LEE: Well, don't abuse that privilege. You want an M&M? I got some in my purse.

HANK: Where's Charlie? He didn't come?

LEE: He has a class in geometry.

HANK: He's already taken remedial geometry.

LEE: This is a make-up class in remedial geometry. *(To the* DOCTOR:*)* Charlie's not doing too well in school.

DR. CHARLOTTE: Mm-hmm.

LEE: They say it's because he reads too much. *(Offering the M&Ms:)* Do you want—

DR. CHARLOTTE: No, thank you.

LEE: So, are you behaving yourself?

HANK: I told you yes.

LEE: All right, I'm just asking.

HANK: So how come you're visiting?

LEE: What do you mean? I don't have to have a reason to visit.

HANK: Then how come you've never visited before?

LEE: I *have* visited before, but you were unconscious.

HANK: That doesn't count as a visit. How can it be a visit if I didn't know you were here?

LEE: I can't be responsible for when you're conscious or unconscious—I can only make the effort.

DR. CHARLOTTE: Mm-hmm.

LEE: Maybe if I knew you were going to be conscious for sure I would visit more often. Do you have some sort of schedule I could take with me?

DR. CHARLOTTE: Your son is off the Thorazine now. You should find him alert most any visiting day.

LEE: See, that's another thing. Saturdays are just about

the worst for me. We're still living in the basement of the church because of our house, and on Saturday I help the nuns—since they took us in I feel I should do something around the place.

DR. CHARLOTTE: Mm-hmm.

LEE: On Saturdays the nuns roll out a sheet of dough and with this shot glass they cut out the—what do you call it?—the body-of-Christ thing they use for their communion. Now I'm not allowed to actually touch the dough, because I'm not a Catholic, but I make sure there's lots of flour spread out on the table so the body-of-Christ thing doesn't stick, because it's hell to clean up. You end up having to scrape it with your nails. And I keep count of how many bodies-of-Christ things they've made.

DR. CHARLOTTE: Communion hosts.

LEE: That's right. It's very relaxing. All the girls get to talking.

(HANK *crosses to leave.* DR. CHARLOTTE *stops him and sits him down.*)

DR. CHARLOTTE: Do you think the nuns would understand if you told them you needed to come visit your son?

LEE: I'm here today, aren't I?

DR. CHARLOTTE: Yes.

(LEE *offers* HANK *a M&M, then puts it in his mouth.*)

LEE: I did come up here to tell you something—your hands are too greasy—though I was planning on coming today anyway.

HANK: What?

LEE: Well, now, it's not good news, but your doctor thinks

it's all right to tell you because, partially, I've got no choice.

HANK: What?

LEE: You know your Aunt Bessie down in Florida. Well, she's got leukemia and I guess she's not doing too well and there's a possibility she might die.

HANK: Who?

LEE: Your Aunt Bessie.

HANK: I didn't know I had an Aunt Bessie.

LEE: Sure you did. My sister. Your aunt. She lives down in Florida.

HANK: This is the first I've heard of her.

LEE: She's been to the house.

HANK: When?

LEE: Right after your dad and I got married.

HANK: I wasn't born yet.

LEE: Oh, I guess you weren't. Well, I know I've mentioned her. She's my sister.

HANK: I didn't know you had a sister.

LEE: You know how at Christmas I always say, "It looks like Bessie didn't send a card this year either"?

HANK: Oh, yeah.

LEE: That's your Aunt Bessie, my sister.

HANK: Okay.

LEE: And she's dying.

HANK: Okay. Are there anymore M&Ms?

LEE: Sure. *(She puts one in his mouth.)* Since we're her nearest relatives they want us to get tested to see if our bone marrow is compatible because they could maybe save her life if they do a bone marrow transplant.

HANK: Yeah?

LEE: They wanted us to fly to Florida but we can't afford that. So we're going to arrange the tests up here and send them down. Okay?

HANK: Why don't we go to Florida?

LEE: Because we don't have any money, Hank. It's a really simple test, they say. And it's not supposed to hurt much.

HANK: What if I don't want to do it?

LEE: What do you mean?

HANK: I don't know her. Why should I let them do anything to me?

LEE: This is my sister we are talking about. And maybe I haven't mentioned her to you before, but that doesn't mean that she isn't on my mind a lot, and we are not going to just let her die because you want to have one of your moods. Do you understand? Now they say they can do your test up here, so . . .

(HANK has walked away and turned his back to her.)

Well, I have to go. It's good to see you, Hank.

HANK: You coming next week?

LEE: I don't know. It's Feast of the Ascension. It gets kind of busy.

DR. CHARLOTTE: Hank, is there anything you want to say to your mother?

LEE: Will it take long? Because I am already late.

HANK: No, I just—well, I'm really sorry I burnt the house down.

LEE: Is that it? 'Cause I am really late. Okay, Hank. Well, you be good now. I'd leave you these *(she indicates the M&Ms)* but they're Charlie's. I just took them with me for the drive. Here, I'll leave you some here. Then when you get cleaned up you can come back for them. *(She pours out some M&Ms onto the seat of the chair.)* Okay, well, we'll see you, and Bessie's doctor should be calling you.

DR. CHARLOTTE: We'll be waiting.

(LEE exits.)

DR. CHARLOTTE: Well . . . *(She takes out a cigarette, lights it, and takes a deep drag.)* Good session.

(Blackout.)

SCENE FIVE

(BESSIE lies in her hospital bed, wearing a wig and eating lunch. RUTH sits in a chair beside her.)

RUTH: Being confined to your bed is nothing to be afraid of.

BESSIE: I'm not confined to my bed. I'm just a little tired today.

RUTH: I was confined to my bed most of my life. You find things to do.

BESSIE: Like what?

RUTH: Oh my . . . well . . . you can sleep, or you can lay there awake. . . .

BESSIE: Do you want any of this?

RUTH: No, no. That's all for you. You eat that and be strong. Have you made a stinky today?

BESSIE: Yes.

RUTH: That's good. That's important. Do you want your rice pudding?

BESSIE: Do you want it?

RUTH: Not if you were going to have it.

BESSIE: You can have it.

RUTH: I didn't really have time for a lunch.

BESSIE: This is too far for you to come, Ruth. I don't think you should visit me again.

RUTH: You visited me every day when I was in for my cure. It's nice for me to visit you.

BESSIE: It's too hard on you.

RUTH: It's such a lovely walk.

BESSIE: Besides, you're needed at home now.

RUTH: I wish we could do something about that garage door. I feel like the whole street knows my business.

BESSIE: How is Dad?

RUTH: Oh, he's fine.

BESSIE: Does he miss me?

RUTH: Well, I haven't actually told him you're gone.

BESSIE: What?

RUTH: I didn't know what to say.

BESSIE: Doesn't he wonder where I am?

RUTH: When he asks, I say you're just in the other room busy with something. Then he falls asleep for a while, and when he wakes up I say he just missed you.

BESSIE: Ruth.

RUTH: It would upset him.

BESSIE: Who does he think that nurse is living with you?

RUTH: Well, I pretend not to notice her.

BESSIE: What do you mean?

RUTH: If she comes in the room while I'm there I pretend she's not real. That she doesn't exist.

BESSIE: Then what does Dad think?

RUTH: I think he thinks he's hallucinating.

BESSIE: What?

RUTH: I never told him he was hallucinating. He came up with that himself. I didn't know what to do. I was going to try to tell him you were in the hospital, and—and she walked in before I was ready, so I didn't. I—I pretended she wasn't there.

BESSIE: You have to tell him.

RUTH: But he's used to it now. The only time it seems to bother him is when she carries him to the bath. And I say, "Oh, look, Marvin, you're flying. Bessie will want to see this." And I go into the other room to get you.

BESSIE: He must think he's losing his mind.

RUTH: But it's better than telling him. You don't know. He would be so upset. He's still your father. What am I supposed to tell him? That his little girl is . . . ? How can I tell him? Then he'll really think he's losing his mind. He'll be so upset. It would be so upsetting to him. He's your father.

BESSIE: All right. All right.

RUTH: I wouldn't know what to say.

BESSIE: Tell him that I'm going to be fine and I'll be home soon and there's no reason to be upset.

RUTH: You want me to tell him?

BESSIE: Yes. Because there is no reason to be upset. I'm going to be fine, Ruth. I know I am.

RUTH: Nothing happens that God doesn't have a reason for.

BESSIE: I'm sure He does.

RUTH: He tries to teach us things. He tries to reach down and shake us out of our ignorance.

BESSIE: I'm sure that's it.

RUTH: I know He made me crippled for a reason. He wants me to learn something. It may be patience or it may be forbearance or it may be how to dress without standing up. He doesn't tell you what it is, you just have to learn it.

BESSIE: I don't think it's how to dress.

RUTH: Oh, it wouldn't surprise me. I often ask Him why I'm crippled. I also ask Him why He let Marvin buy

this house down here to take care of me, then struck
Marvin with a stroke. Why? And then have him lose
his colon to cancer. Why? And then lose the sight in
one eye and the use of one kidney and yet keep a full
head of hair. Why?

BESSIE: I don't know.

RUTH: But God knows. He has his reasons. And I'm not
upset.

BESSIE: Then tell Dad his nurse is not a hallucination and
that I am not in the other room.

RUTH: I think he's starting to enjoy flying.

BESSIE: And I don't want you to visit me again. It's too
hard on you. (Pause.) It's almost time for your show.
Don't you want to watch?

RUTH: I didn't think you would want to.

BESSIE: I kind of want to see if Lance proposes to Coral.

RUTH: Have you been watching?

BESSIE: I've seen it since I've been in here.

RUTH (sits on the bed with BESSIE): Isn't it wonderful?
I think she'll say yes. They really do love each other.

BESSIE: But now, is he the same guy who raped her at
one point?

RUTH: Oh, that was months ago. He's really a nice boy.

(BESSIE clicks on the TV with the remote. She and
RUTH both look to the corner of the room where it would
be. The soap opera theme swells as the lights fade.)

SCENE SIX

(Bessie's home. BESSIE is in Marvin's room.)

BESSIE *(from Marvin's room)*: Okay, Dad. Roll that way.
Let me get the sheet. Oh, c'mon, you can help me out
a little bit.

(The doorbell rings.)
(LEE enters with suitcases.)

Ruth! Dad, now I need to get that side of the sheet
too, so would you roll toward me now? Just a little.
LEE: Hello?
BESSIE: Lee?
LEE: Bessie?
BESSIE: I'll be right out. *(To MARVIN:)* Now you'll be
okay for a moment. I've just got to put these to soak.

(BESSIE enters, carrying balled-up sheets.)

LEE: Bessie. I rang the bell.

BESSIE: Didn't Ruth let you in?

LEE: No, she—

(BESSIE'S and LEE'S statements overlap.)

BESSIE: Well, I don't know where she got to. She's probably in front of the TV somewhere. I told her to keep an eye out for you.

LEE: That's all right. She probably just didn't hear the bell. I just let myself in. I hope you don't mind.

BESSIE: Not at all. Look at you.

LEE: What?

BESSIE: Look at you. Are you that old? How old does that make me, then?

LEE: Why, do I look old?

BESSIE: Well, you're a lot older.

LEE: You look good, though, Bessie. You really do. I like your hair.

BESSIE: This is a wig. It's from my chemo.

LEE: Oh. *(Slight pause.)* I know it's a wig. I don't know why I pretended I didn't. Not that it looks like a wig.

BESSIE: Thanks.

LEE: I'm wearing a fall. Isn't that something? I've always loved this length, but I've never had the patience for it. I just wear it when I want to look nice.

BESSIE: Why don't you sit down? I've got to put these to soak. Dad had himself a little accident.

LEE: Oh. How is he?

BESSIE: He's still with us.

LEE: Let me help.

BESSIE: No, no. You sit down. This will only take a second.

(She exits.)

(LEE *stands by the entrance to Marvin's room and lights cigarette.*)

LEE: Daddy? It's me, Lee. All the way down from Ohio. We came after all. (*Pause.*) The nuns had a big bake sale for us to pay for our way down here. Can I come in? (*She goes in.*) Hi, Daddy. (*She returns, slightly upset.*)

(BESSIE *enters.*)

BESSIE: I let them soak and worry about them later. Oh, Lee, I don't know if you should smoke in the house.

LEE: Oh, I'm—

BESSIE: No, you could smoke in the garage if you—

LEE: No, no.

BESSIE: Dad's oxygen tanks.

LEE: I understand.

BESSIE: Or you could smoke in the yard.

LEE: I don't have to smoke.

BESSIE: Where're your boys? Couldn't you get Hank out of the mental institution?

LEE: Bessie, we don't like to call it the mental institution.

BESSIE: What do you call it?

LEE: We call it the loony bin or the nuthouse, to show we've got a sense of humor about it.

BESSIE: Well, where is he? Where's Charlie? I've got myself two grown nephews I've never seen.

LEE: Now, I invited you up for both their christenings.

BESSIE: I've got my hands full down here.

LEE: Who stayed while you were in the hospital?

BESSIE: We had a nurse come in.

LEE: That must have been expensive. I want to write you a check.

BESSIE: Oh, no. That's all right.

LEE (*writing check*): Don't worry. It's not going to be much.

BESSIE: That's okay, Lee. We've gotten by this long. We're glad you're here now.

LEE: Of course I'm here. You're my sister.

BESSIE: Where are your boys?

LEE: They're sitting out in the car.

BESSIE: The car? Why don't they come in?

LEE: You have to ask Hank that.

BESSIE: Do they need help with their stuff?

LEE: He's just doing this to make me mad.

BESSIE: Should we—?

LEE: Don't worry about it. I know how to handle Hank. He won't cause you a problem while he's here.

BESSIE: You probably want to see Dad. It's been such a long time.

LEE: Sure.

BESSIE: Well, let me get him dressed and cleaned up a little. He wouldn't want you to see him like he is.

LEE: You sure I can't help?

BESSIE: I've been doing it this long.

(BESSIE *exits into Marvin's room.* RUTH *enters.*)

LEE: Aunt Ruth?

RUTH: Oh, look who it is! And isn't she pretty!

LEE: Aunt Ruth?

RUTH: You remember an old thing like me?

LEE: You're up and about.

RUTH: Oh, I've got my cure. I'm part machine. I hope you don't think I'm rude, but I'm watching my show and I just hate to miss it. I knew you'd come right when it starts.

LEE: Oh, no, you watch your program.

RUTH: Are you going to give me a hug?

(LEE hugs RUTH.)

Give me a real hug. I won't break.

(LEE hugs RUTH harder. This hurts RUTH.)

Oh, Jesus. Oh, sweet Jesus. Oh, Jesus.

(RUTH turns her dial. The garage door is heard going up.)

LEE: Oh I'm sorry. I'm sorry. Here—sit.

(BESSIE enters.)

BESSIE: I heard the garage door.
RUTH: Lee hurt my back.
LEE: I didn't mean to.
BESSIE: I'm sure she didn't mean to.
RUTH: I know she didn't mean to. She's a sweet girl.
LEE: I brought some cookies left over from the bake sale.
RUTH: Isn't that thoughtful. But I'm not allowed sugar.
LEE: But you'll like them, Bessie. Seven-layer cookies.
BESSIE: Thanks, Lee, but I'm trying to stay away from
    that stuff now too.
LEE: Does Dad still have a sweet tooth?
BESSIE: You bet.
LEE: That's good.
BESSIE: Which makes his diabetes all the more frustrating.
LEE: Diabetes?
RUTH: But it's a lovely canister, isn't it.
BESSIE: Do you want to see Dad?
LEE: Sure.
RUTH: Who are those two boys sitting in the car in the
    driveway?

LEE: That's Hank and Charlie. This is something I need to tell you both.

RUTH: I think the commercial break must be over. Could you tell me later?

LEE: Oh, sure.

(*RUTH exits.*)

Bessie, Hank will do things like this to get attention. They say I just have to ignore it. Or give him an ultimatum.

BESSIE: What about Charlie?

LEE: He just goes along with Hank. Or he might be reading.

BESSIE: What if I ask them in?

LEE: No. If we ask them in, I have to be prepared to *make* him come in. I don't feel up to it.

BESSIE: Oh, now.

LEE: He just wants the attention. He hasn't agreed to be tested for the transplant yet because he knows he'll be the center of attention. You have to ignore him.

BESSIE: He hasn't?

LEE: Oh, but don't worry. He will.

BESSIE: We can't have him do anything he doesn't want to.

LEE: No. He will. I'll make him if I have to.

BESSIE: How are you going to make him, Lee? You can't make him come in from the drive.

(*Pause. LEE exits. BESSIE sees the check, picks it up, tears it up, and puts the pieces back on the counter.*)
(*RUTH enters.*)

RUTH: I keep missing the show and only catch the commercials.

BESSIE: You're supposed to watch. You're supposed to tell me what happens.

(LEE enters.)

LEE: Can I use your phone?
BESSIE: Sure.
LEE: Do you have the number for the police?

(BESSIE and RUTH answer simultaneously.)

BESSIE: Why? What happened?
RUTH: Oh, my!
LEE: Nothing's happened. I had to give Hank an ultimatum. That's what his doctor told me I'm supposed to do—clearly define the rules so Hank knows what the consequences are.
BESSIE: Couldn't you tell him no more TV?
LEE: He burned the TV.
RUTH: Are they smoking drugs out there?
LEE: Do you have the number?
BESSIE: This seems extreme.
LEE: Just give me the number, Bessie.
BESSIE: Here's a list of emergency numbers. It's right there under Chicken Delivery.
LEE: Thank you. I'm sorry about this. *(She dials.)*
RUTH: Coral told Storm she is going to marry Lance.
BESSIE: Tell me later, Ruth, okay?

(HANK and CHARLIE enter. CHARLIE—twelve years old, thick glasses, hard shoes—engrossed in a book.)

HANK: Hey.
BESSIE: Well, look who's here.
LEE: Thank you for coming in, Hank.

HANK: We were coming in, Mom. They were doing a Top Ten countdown and we wanted to hear number one.

LEE: Why didn't you say that?

HANK: I don't know. You were shouting and everything. It just didn't seem like the time.

LEE: You're trying to make me look bad in front of your aunts and they see right through it.

BESSIE: Well, you're here. And I'm your Aunt Bessie who you have never laid eyes on, but I don't care if you are all grown up, I expect a big, fat hug.

HANK: Sure. *(He hugs* BESSIE.)

RUTH: I'm Ruth.

(HANK hugs RUTH.)

RUTH: Oh, Jesus. Oh, sweet Jesus. Oh, Jesus.

(She turns her dial. The garage door is heard.)

HANK: What'd I do? What'd I do? I'm sorry.

RUTH: That damn garage. Driving me nuts.

BESSIE: Sit down, Ruth.

RUTH: I'm fine.

BESSIE: And you must be Charlie. Do you have a hug for your Aunt Bessie?

(CHARLIE hugs her.)

RUTH: And I'm Ruth, your great aunt.

(CHARLIE extends his hand to her.)

Thank you. Which one of you handsome boys is in the mental institution?

BESSIE: She means the loony bin.

HANK: That's me.
BESSIE: Do you all want to go in and see Dad?
HANK: Sure.
RUTH: Marvin! Company's coming! Company's coming!
BESSIE: I know he's excited about meeting all of you.

(They go in. MARVIN is heard muttering.)

Dad, it's Lee, your daughter, and these are her boys,
your grandkids. . . . No, don't be scared. They're real.
They're real . . . Maybe this is too much right now.

(They leave the room. RUTH stays inside.)

RUTH *(from Marvin's room)*: Don't be scared of your own
   grandkids.
BESSIE: It's just too much excitement.
LEE: Should you be taking it easy?
BESSIE: I'm fine. I seem to be in remission, which is the
   best time for a transplant. I want to thank you all for
   coming down here and for helping me out. It's a lot to
   ask of someone to donate their bone marrow.
CHARLIE: I think it sounds neat.
BESSIE: But I could understand if someone were to be
   reluctant.
HANK: I'm thinking about it, that's all.
BESSIE: Lee, your appointment is today at three. I hope
   you don't feel rushed.
LEE: No.
BESSIE: The odds are better that your mother will be a
   match, so she'll get tested first and then maybe you kids
   won't have to bother.
CHARLIE *(disappointed)*: Really?

(HANK picks a potato chip out of a bowl.)

LEE: Hank, did Bessie offer you a chip yet?

BESSIE: Oh, that's what they're there for.

LEE: He has to wait to be asked, Bessie. Put the chip back, Hank.

(Pause.)

Put it back.

(Pause.)

Put back the chip.

(Pause. LEE crumbles the chip in HANK's hand.)

BESSIE: Lee, I put them out for the kids.

LEE: You have to understand—he has to wait to be asked.

BESSIE: Hank, would you like a chip?

HANK: No, thank you, Aunt Bessie. Not right now.

LEE: Your aunt offered you a chip—the polite thing to do would be to take it.

HANK: I don't want one right now.

LEE: Eat a chip or no Disney World.

HANK: I could give a fuck about Disney World.

LEE: That's it. Get out of my sight. I don't care where. Just so I can't see you.

(HANK exits the house. Pause.)

BESSIE: Charlie, would you like a chip?

(CHARLIE looks at his mom.)

LEE: Go ahead, honey, if you want one.

BESSIE: Take a bunch.

(CHARLIE *grabs a handful.*)

LEE: Not too many. You'll spoil your lunch.

(CHARLIE *puts them all back but one. He is about to bite it.*)

LEE: Don't make crumbs on your aunt's nice floor.

(CHARLIE *sucks on the chip. Pause.*)

CHARLIE: Can I go watch Grandpa breathe?
LEE: Charlie, don't word things that way.
BESSIE: Sure you can.

(CHARLIE *exits to Marvin's room.*)

RUTH (*from Marvin's room*): Look who it is, Marvin. It's Charlie. . . . No, he's real. Here, Charlie. Do this.

(*The light starts bouncing on Marvin's wall.*)

LEE: Bessie, I'm sorry about all this. You should have quiet and I'm—I'm sorry. But this is what the doctor has asked me to do. I'm at the end of my rope. (*Sees the check.*) You tore up my check?
BESSIE: Lee, I'm glad you're here, but we've been getting along fine by ourselves for a long time and not because we've wanted to. That was your choice. Please, I'm glad to see you. I'm very grateful, but we're doing okay.

(*Pause.*)

LEE (*looking out the window*): Hank, I can see you!!

(*Blackout.*)

SCENE SEVEN

(Late at night in the backyard. HANK is examining tools in an old toolbox. BESSIE enters with a cup of coffee.)

BESSIE: Hank? . . . Hank, is that you?
HANK: Yeah.
BESSIE: What are you doing out here?
HANK: Nothing.
BESSIE: It's kind of late to be up doing nothing.
HANK: What are you doing?
BESSIE: I'm having some coffee. Can't you sleep?
HANK: I don't need much sleep.
BESSIE: Growing boys need their sleep.
HANK: I'm done growing.
BESSIE: Do you want a sip of my coffee, then?
HANK: No.
BESSIE: You gave me a scare, Hank. I'm not used to finding someone else back here.
HANK: You want me to go inside?
BESSIE: No. Unless . . . Are you not supposed to be out here? Will your mom care?

HANK: She's asleep.

BESSIE: I don't see any harm in it. But don't tell your Aunt Ruth that I wander away from the house at night. It might make her nervous.

HANK: She's not my aunt.

BESSIE: Sure she is.

HANK: She's my great aunt. You're my aunt. Marvin's my grandfather. I got a whole new family.

BESSIE: I guess you do. Must seem kind of strange.

HANK: No stranger than anything else.

BESSIE: We're all glad you're here.

HANK: Yeah, we should do it again in another seventeen years.

(Pause.)

BESSIE: Do you like Florida so far?

HANK: Haven't seen much.

BESSIE: Nights like this are nice. You used to be able to see just a patch of the gulf right through there.

HANK: Where?

BESSIE: You can't anymore. They built that elementary school. I don't know where they thought the kids would come from. You can still smell the water, though.

HANK: I can't.

BESSIE: You can't? Maybe I just remember smelling it.

(Pause.)

Your mom and I haven't always gotten along. That's why I haven't been in touch so much.

HANK: Uh-huh.

BESSIE: You sure did a lot of hard work around here this afternoon.

HANK: I was bored.

BESSIE: I knew Dad's respirator shouldn't rattle like that.

HANK: You just had to get those Monopoly hotels that were crammed in there loose.

BESSIE: I wish you could have really known your grandfather. He'd a liked having a boy around.

HANK: He was kind of jabbering at me when I was there.

BESSIE: That's his way of talking to you.

HANK: Kind of gave me the creeps.

BESSIE: Well, he's been sick for a very long time.

HANK: Don't you ever wish he would just die?

BESSIE: Hank . . . Don't ask that.

HANK: Why not?

BESSIE: It's rude.

HANK: I haven't made up my mind about getting tested yet.

BESSIE: Hopefully your mom will be a match.

HANK: Even if she isn't, I just . . .

BESSIE: Is that what you were doing? Sitting out here thinking about it?

HANK: No.

BESSIE: Oh. What were you thinking about?

(Pause.)

You don't have to tell me, of course.

(Pause.)

What are you doing with the tools?

HANK: I'm just looking at them. I was going to put them back.

BESSIE: I didn't think you were stealing them, Hank. You can have them if you want.

HANK: Really?

BESSIE: Sure.

HANK: You're giving them to me?

BESSIE: Sure.

HANK: You're just giving them to me?

BESSIE: Sure, why not?

HANK: These are really cool tools.

BESSIE: Are they?

HANK: Yeah, they're ancient.

BESSIE: That used to be your grandfather's toolbox. I think he'd like you to have it.

HANK: They won't let me keep these, though.

BESSIE: Who won't?

HANK: The hospital.

BESSIE: Well, you won't be in there forever.

HANK: When I go back they're moving me to a place for adults.

BESSIE: Why?

HANK: I turn eighteen in three weeks.

BESSIE: Oh. Happy birthday.

HANK: Thanks. If the fire hadn't spread up the street it wouldn't be such a big deal.

BESSIE: Uh-huh.

HANK: Or if melting plastic didn't give off noxious fumes. Now they want to be sure I'm not a threat.

BESSIE: You're not a threat. I'm sure they'll see that. You're probably the best one there.

HANK: There's this one dude on my floor held a razor blade under his tongue for five hours. Talked to the orderlies and ate and everything.

BESSIE: Why on earth would he do that?

HANK: He was trying to break my record.

BESSIE: Hank. What do you want to be when you grow up?

HANK: I am grown up.

BESSIE: When I look at you I see a lost little boy.

HANK: Then get your eyes checked.

(Pause.)

So Marvin liked to fix stuff?

BESSIE: Maybe that's where you get it from. He used to make your mom so mad. He'd leave the radio lying in pieces. She liked to turn it up and dance wild around the house.

HANK: Mom liked to dance?

BESSIE: You bet.

HANK *(taking a photograph from the toolbox)*: Hey, who is this?

BESSIE: Let me see.

(She and HANK look at the photo together.)

That's your grandmother.

HANK: Looks kind of like Mom.

BESSIE: She takes after her. Your grandfather used to have this taped above his workbench.

HANK: She's young.

BESSIE: She *was* young. *(Indicating the photo:)* Do you want this too?

HANK: I don't care.

BESSIE: Then I'll keep it.

HANK: Did you know my dad?

BESSIE: I met him once. Doesn't your mom talk about him?

HANK: I know he had a motorcycle.

BESSIE: Did he?

HANK: Yeah.

BESSIE: I know your mom was nuts about him.

HANK: Did you meet him at the wedding?

BESSIE: No. It was when I pretty much knew that I was going to be down here with Dad and Ruth for longer than I thought. So I went back home to sell off the rest of my stuff.

HANK: They have you over for dinner or something?

BESSIE: No. I just sort of stopped by. I was curious to see this guy who could take up absolutely all of your mother's time. It wasn't much of a visit. He was asleep on the couch. Lee didn't want to wake him up, and she had just mopped the kitchen floor, so we stood in the hallway and talked for a while. When I left he was still asleep.

HANK: How'd he seem?

BESSIE: He seemed nice enough.

HANK: I don't think I'll get the test. What do you think about that?

BESSIE: Can I ask why?

HANK: No reason.

(Pause.)

Being outside here is different than being outside at the hospital.

BESSIE: How?

HANK: Seems bigger.

BESSIE: Maybe your mom wouldn't want you out this late.

HANK: Okay.

BESSIE: Did Ruth thank you for fixing the garage door?

HANK: Yeah.

BESSIE: That was very nice of you.

HANK: Nobody ever does anything to be nice. That's what my therapist says.

BESSIE: He does?

HANK: People don't just do things. They get something for it.

BESSIE: He says that?

HANK: Yeah.

BESSIE: And you believe him?

HANK: Yeah.

BESSIE: Why have I spent the last twenty years of my life down here? Because I enjoyed it? Because I got something out of it?

HANK: Yeah, or you wouldn't do it.

BESSIE: No, Hank, no. Sometimes I can barely . . . No.

HANK: First time I hear from you is when you need something.

BESSIE: Hank—

HANK: Maybe you did it because maybe you thought you'd never land a husband. Or maybe you just wanted to hide out. When you're not around a nursing home will do it for the cash.

BESSIE: Your mom wouldn't let them go to a home.

HANK: Why not? She doesn't give a shit about anybody.

LEE (off): Hank! Hank!

HANK (indicating the tools): Where do you want me to put these?

BESSIE: They're yours.

HANK: Okay. (He starts to go.)

BESSIE: Hank. You're my nephew and I love you no matter what you've decided.

(Pause.)

HANK: Okay.

(He exits.)

(BESSIE stands alone as the lights fade to black.)

ACT TWO
SCENE ONE

(BESSIE and LEE wait in the consulting room of a retirement home. A bowl of candies sits on a table.)

BESSIE: What's the time?
LEE: You just asked me.
BESSIE: What is it?
LEE: Four-twelve. *(Pause.)* Are you tired?
BESSIE: No. *(Slight pause.)* Why? Do I look tired?
LEE: You look good.
BESSIE: Then why did you ask me?
LEE: We've been waiting. I thought maybe you were tired of waiting.
BESSIE: I am tired of waiting.
LEE: That's all I meant. *(Pause.)* Why? Do you feel tired?
BESSIE: I feel fine.
LEE: You look great.
BESSIE: I feel good.

(The RETIREMENT HOME DIRECTOR enters and joins BESSIE and LEE.)

DIRECTOR: Let me try to explain it again.

LEE: I understood what you were saying.

DIRECTOR: Then for your sister's benefit.

BESSIE: You're saying I couldn't afford to put Dad and Ruth in this nursing home even if I wanted to.

DIRECTOR: That's not what I'm saying.

LEE: It's not?

DIRECTOR: No.

LEE: What are you saying?

DIRECTOR: Let me say this—what does it matter what I'm saying if you have no interest in this institution?

LEE: I didn't say that.

DIRECTOR: She did.

LEE: She didn't mean it.

BESSIE: I think I did.

LEE: Where do you want them to end up, Bessie? At County? For recreation they push the wheelchairs into the hall and let you watch the medicine carts roll by. Here they have computer games. They have Nerf basketball.

DIRECTOR: We have a video library. Sing-alongs. Date nights.

BESSIE: Who is Dad going to date?

DIRECTOR: You'd be surprised. Women outnumber the men five to one.

LEE: This is the best place we've seen.

BESSIE: We can't afford it, so why are we talking?

DIRECTOR: I never said that.

BESSIE: What did you say?

DIRECTOR: Let me get something that might help.

(The DIRECTOR *exits.)*

LEE: I know this is hard. There's no reason to be depressed about my test results, because I know Charlie

is bound to match. So none of this means anything any-
way, because you're going to be fine.
BESSIE: I don't like you pressuring Hank.
LEE: What I'd like to do is take a stick to him.

(Pause.)

BESSIE: I have to take Charlie to Dr. Wally's and still get
to the pharmacy before it closes.
LEE: I'll take Charlie. We've got time. You've got more
energy than I do. The way you handle Daddy and Ruth
. . . I wouldn't last a week.
BESSIE: It's not hard.
LEE: You've done amazing things, Bessie.
BESSIE: I haven't done so much.
LEE: You should be proud.
BESSIE: I just did what anybody would do.
LEE: I get my degree next quarter.
BESSIE: You should be proud of that.
LEE: I already had one free-lance job doing hair for a TV
commercial. It was just local, but guess how much they
paid for one day.
BESSIE: I don't feel like guessing.
LEE: Guess.
BESSIE: Three hundred dollars.
LEE *(disappointed)*: That's right. Three hundred dollars.
Why did you guess that?
BESSIE: It just popped into my head.
LEE: Most people would have guessed lower.
BESSIE: Three hundred dollars is a lot of money.
LEE: It's a lot for one day. I feel like my life is finally
starting.
BESSIE: Who would take care of them here?
LEE: Doctors. Did you see they have a pool? They have

a mirror ball in the cafeteria for disco night. This is a nice place. It even smells nice. Do you want a candy?

BESSIE: No.

LEE: I should take them all. She's kept us waiting so long. Serve her right. I could give them to the boys.

BESSIE: Don't steal them. She'll notice they're gone.

LEE: She's not going to accuse us. She'd be too embarrassed. *(She dumps the candies into her purse.)*

BESSIE: Lee!

LEE: Relax or she'll think you took them.

BESSIE: Put them back.

LEE: I can't. They're all rolling around in my purse.

(The DIRECTOR re-enters with papers in hand.)

DIRECTOR: All right. *(She gives papers to BESSIE and to LEE.)* If you turn to page four, you'll see a chart for the various state and national financial aid programs for this institution. Do you see that? Page four.

BESSIE: I have the low-impact aerobic schedule.

LEE: So do I.

DIRECTOR: Here.

(She takes back the papers and exits.)

BESSIE: Is the woman at the front desk a nurse?

LEE: She was wearing white.

BESSIE: They do that so you'll think there are more nurses around than there are. Did you touch her hands?

LEE: Why would I touch her hands?

BESSIE: They're ice. She has no circulation. I can't believe they let her touch patients.

LEE: She's probably just a receptionist.

BESSIE: So she's a fake.

LEE: She's not a fake. She's a real receptionist dressed in white.

BESSIE: Dad would have never done this.

LEE: Well . . .

BESSIE: Do you remember how he cared for Mom?

LEE: I was little. Mom was just this vague presence in a shut room at the end of the hall.

BESSIE: I remember.

LEE: We're doing the mature thing. We're seeing what our options are.

BESSIE: Why can't *you* take Dad and Ruth?

LEE: The nuns would love that.

BESSIE: You could move down here. You could have the house.

LEE: I don't think so.

BESSIE: Why not?

LEE: I've got Hank to think about.

BESSIE: He's very unhappy there.

LEE: Of course he's unhappy there. If he were happy he wouldn't be there.

BESSIE: You could find a nice place for him here, Lee. You'd have the whole house. The sunshine. You could find work down here.

LEE: No.

BESSIE: Give me one good reason.

LEE: Just no.

BESSIE: Why?

LEE: Because I don't want to.

(Pause.)

I made this decision once already. When Daddy had his first stroke—I made this decision then. I wasn't going to waste my life.

BESSIE: You think I've wasted my life?

LEE: Of course not.

BESSIE: I can't imagine a better way to have spent my life.

LEE: Then we both made the right decision.

BESSIE: You are the most . . .

LEE: Say it. You've been saying it a million different ways since I got down here.

BESSIE: I have not. I have bent over backwards to avoid having this conversation with you.

LEE: What conversation?

(Pause.)

(BESSIE opens her purse and puts about a dollar's change in the candy bowl.)

LEE: What are you doing?

BESSIE: I'm paying for them.

LEE: Put that back.

BESSIE: I'm not going to steal them. It's wrong.

LEE: It's not wrong.

BESSIE: Wrong is wrong.

LEE: It's your money.

(The DIRECTOR re-enters with more papers and hands them to BESSIE and to LEE.)

DIRECTOR: Turn to page four. You'll see a chart of the various financial aid programs available.

LEE and BESSIE *(simultaneously)*: Uh-huh.

DIRECTOR: And you'll see that you don't qualify for any of them.

BESSIE: So you're wasting our time.

DIRECTOR: No. It means you have to drop into a lower income bracket.

BESSIE: Lower?

DIRECTOR: You need to deplete your savings on nonasset acquisitions. Including your home equity.

BESSIE: Lower?

DIRECTOR: Let me explain it again.

LEE: I understand.

DIRECTOR: Then for your sister's benefit. You need to spend your savings and your home equity on something that has no resale value and cannot be considered an asset. Seventy percent of our residents have done this to qualify for assistance.

LEE: What do they buy?

DIRECTOR: Most buy very elaborate tombstones. It's the perfect financial solution.

(Pause.)

BESSIE: I'm going to wait in the car.

(She exits.)
(Pause.)

LEE: Do you have something I could take with me?

(The DIRECTOR reaches to pick up a brochure off the table, sees the money in the candy bowl, and looks at LEE.)

(Blackout.)

SCENE TWO

(The doctor's waiting room. HANK and CHARLIE sit in chairs near each other. DR. WALLY faces them. BOB stands by.)

DR. WALLY: Is everyone clear on the procedure we are about to do? Are there any questions?
BOB: How long does the anesthetic take to work?
DR. WALLY: It's not so important that *you* understand the procedure, Bob.
BOB: Could I have your medical history cards, please?

(HANK and CHARLIE give them to him.)

DR. WALLY: Who is going to be the brave one and go first?
CHARLIE: I want to go first. Can I?
HANK: I don't care.

(DR. WALLY and CHARLIE start out.)

DR. WALLY: What grade are you in now, Hank?

CHARLIE: I'm Charlie.
DR. WALLY: I'm Dr. Wally.

(They exit.)

BOB: Hank, am I reading your medical card correctly? Are you currently on lithium?
HANK: Yeah.
BOB: It's a great drug, isn't it?
HANK: Uh . . .
BOB: Can I ask you something? Did you find you put on a lot of weight since?
HANK: No.
BOB: No? Hmmm.

(He exits.)
(BESSIE enters.)

BESSIE: Hank. I thought you'd be at home.
HANK: No, I'm here.
BESSIE: Where's your mom?
HANK: She went over to the mall.
BESSIE: Where's Charlie?
HANK: He's in back already.
BESSIE: Are you here to be with Charlie?
HANK: I'll probably get tested too.
BESSIE: Nervous?
HANK: No.
BESSIE: These are new offices for them. Their old one became infested with bugs.
HANK: Bugs don't bother me.
BESSIE: No?
HANK: They crawl out of the drain in the boys' shower. They hide in the lumber in the wood shop. They float in the soap basins on the sinks. You get used to them.

BESSIE: I wouldn't.

HANK: One dude in my room—there's twelve of us in this room, and this one dude catches bugs and puts them on a leash.

BESSIE: A leash?

HANK: A hair leash. He pulls out a strand of his hair and ties it around the bug and the other end he tacks down under his bunk. He had this whole zoo of bugs walking in little circles under his bed.

BESSIE: Hank.

HANK: Till this other dude smashed them all with the back of this cafeteria tray. It was funny.

BESSIE: Sounds funny.

HANK: It's not like anybody ate off the tray. It was an old tray. We use it to slide down the mud hill behind the seizure ward.

BESSIE: Uh-huh.

HANK: You get going real fast. This one dude's old man used to clock pitches for the National League East. He clocked me with his radar gun going fifty.

BESSIE: That's fast.

HANK: And my tray shot out from underneath me and broke this dude's windpipe. We had to perform an emergency tracheotomy with a sharp piece of bark and a Bic pen.

BESSIE: Hmmm.

HANK: Man, it was something. You want a candy? *(He offers her a candy from the nursing home.)*

BESSIE: No. Why do you make up these stories?

HANK: What?

BESSIE: These stories. Razors under the tongue, tracheotomies.

HANK: I'm not making anything up.

BESSIE: Why did you pretend you weren't going to get tested? Why did you put me through that?

HANK: I could still walk out of here.

BESSIE: Why do you tell so many lies?

HANK: I haven't told you shit. You don't know anything about that place.

BESSIE: Then tell me.

HANK: You don't know.

BESSIE: Tell me.

(Long pause.)

HANK: You don't know.

BESSIE: I was in the hospital. It was boring. I was scared and it was boring.

HANK: There's this one dude—

BESSIE: If this is another tall tale I'm not interested. *(She picks up a magazine.)*

HANK *(sits)*: Toss me one, okay?

(BESSIE gives him a magazine. They flip through them.)

HANK *(looking at a picture)*: Man, what magazine is this? *(He checks the cover and returns to picture.)* That's a human heart.

(BESSIE pays him no attention.)

That's a kidney. . . . That's a lung. . . . That's a brain. . . . That's the eye. . . . That's skin. *(Pause.)* I played in a pool tournament in my ward. Did Mom tell you?

BESSIE: No.

HANK: I came in fourth. It's true. She doesn't think it's a big deal.

BESSIE: That's great.

(Slight pause.)

HANK: I got my toe broken in there.

BESSIE: How?

HANK: Guy threw a garbage can at me and it landed on my foot.

BESSIE: Why'd he do that?

HANK: No reason I know of. Broken toes never heal.

BESSIE: Does it hurt?

HANK: Sometimes. *(Slight pause.)* A lot of drugs float around in there.

BESSIE: Do you take them?

HANK: Most of the time I keep to myself. Most of the time I sit in my room. I've got a roommate, but most of the time he's got his face to the wall. Most of the time I think about not being there. I think what would it be like to be someone else. Someone I see on the TV or in a magazine, or even walking free on the grounds. They can keep me as long as they want. It's not like a prison term. I've already been there longer than most. A lot of the time I think about getting this house with all this land around it. And I'd get a bunch of dogs—not little ones you might step on but big dogs, like a horse—and I'd let them run wild. They'd never know a leash. And I'd build a go-cart track on my property. Charge people to race around on it. Those places pull in the bucks. I'd be raking it in. And nobody would know where I was. I'd be gone. Most of the time I just want to be someplace else.

BESSIE: Why aren't you?

HANK: Huh?

BESSIE: Why aren't you someplace else?

HANK: What do you mean?

BESSIE: Do you want to be in there?

HANK: No way.

BESSIE: Then why are you?

HANK: I've got no choice.

BESSIE: You're the one who told me people only do what
  they want.
HANK: Yeah.
BESSIE: So you must want to be there.
HANK: No. No way.
BESSIE: Then show them you don't need to be in there.
HANK: It's not easy like that. People start thinking of you
  in a certain way and pretty soon you're that way.
BESSIE: So there's nothing you can do?
HANK: It's hard, that's all.
BESSIE: I don't want you wasting your life in there.
HANK: Neither do I.
BESSIE: Then why are you still there?
HANK: They put me there.
BESSIE: Why'd they put you there?
HANK: 'Cause I burned down the house.
BESSIE: Why'd you burn down the house?

(Slight pause.)
(DR. WALLY enters.)

DR. WALLY: Hank, do you want to come on back? We can
  get you started while we're waiting for the anesthetic to
  start working on little Sammy.
HANK: Charlie.
DR. WALLY: I'm sorry. Did I call you Hank? It's these
  new offices. Do you want to come back?

(He exits.)

HANK: Would you come back with me?
BESSIE: Sure I would.

(They exit.)

(Blackout.)

SCENE THREE

(Bessie's home. Night. CHARLIE and HANK on the floor in sleeping bags.)

CHARLIE *(after a moment, sitting up)*: Hank?
HANK: Yeah.
CHARLIE: Do you ever think about actually dying?

(Pause.)

HANK: No. Do you?
CHARLIE: No. *(Pause.)* Hank, what do you want for your
    birthday?
HANK: I don't care.
CHARLIE: I wish we never had to go home. *(He pulls the
    sleeping bag up over his head.)*
HANK: Can you breathe like that?
CHARLIE: Yeah. *(Pause.)* Hank?
HANK: Yeah.
CHARLIE: Are you excited about Walt Disney World?

(Pause.)

HANK: Yeah. Are you?
CHARLIE: Yeah.

(Lights fade on CHARLIE and HANK as BESSIE enters the kitchen area. BESSIE pours herself coffee. The only light we see is when she opens the refrigerator to get out the cream. After a while, LEE enters in the dark. She turns on the light. BESSIE is standing there without her wig, frozen for a moment, like a rabbit caught in a car's headlights.)

LEE: Oh.
BESSIE: I was just going to bed.

(She exits.)
(LEE pours juice and vodka into a glass.)
(BESSIE re-enters, wearing her wig.)

BESSIE: Forgot my coffee.
LEE: Why are you drinking coffee so late?
BESSIE: I like it. Why are you up?
LEE: I guess I was thirsty.
BESSIE: Did you find everything you need?
LEE: Yes. Thank you.
BESSIE: You're welcome. The boys didn't eat much at dinner.
LEE: No. You have a way with Hank.
BESSIE: I don't.
LEE: You do. You have a way with him.
BESSIE: He's a good boy.
LEE: Is he?
BESSIE: Sure he is.
LEE: I wish I knew your secret.
BESSIE: I just talk to him.

LEE: Are you saying I don't?

(Slight pause.)

BESSIE *(starting to exit)*: I'm tired and we've got Disney World tomorrow.

LEE: You know, I could fix your wig for you.

BESSIE: Fix it?

LEE: I could style it for you. I know how.

BESSIE: Does it look bad?

LEE: No, but if you've got a wig you should have fun with it. Try different looks.

BESSIE: Uh-huh.

LEE: Something sporty, or a sophisticated, out-on-the-town evening thing.

BESSIE: I just brush it out now and then.

LEE: I've got a whole makeup kit down here too.

BESSIE: I don't bother with that much.

LEE: You should. I mean because it's fun. And you never know when you might meet someone.

BESSIE: Meet someone?

LEE: Sure.

BESSIE: A man?

LEE: Yes, a man.

BESSIE: I haven't thought about a man in years.

LEE: You're lying.

BESSIE: I'm sorry we haven't been seeing eye to eye.

LEE: When?

BESSIE: At the nursing home.

LEE: I don't remember anything about it.

BESSIE: I don't want us to fight.

LEE: I don't think we have been.

BESSIE: I want us to get along.

LEE: We do get along.

BESSIE: I don't want us to just get along. I don't want us
   to be polite.
LEE: I've never had a problem with that.
BESSIE: I want us to . . . I want . . . *(Pause.)* Not much
   seems important to me now.
LEE: We're sisters.
BESSIE: The past is—
LEE: We're sisters.
BESSIE: I want you to know—
LEE: I do know.

(MARVIN stirs in his room.)

   Should we . . . ?
BESSIE: Just sit quiet for a moment. He scares himself
   sometimes. He'll go back to sleep.

(They're quiet.)

LEE: Do you remember when Daddy used to drive us
   down to Miami for vacations?
BESSIE: Sure I do. The two of us asleep in the backseat.
LEE: How'd we fit?
BESSIE: Tuna sandwiches sliding across the dash.
LEE: Daddy had the talk radio on real low.
BESSIE: It'd be so cold outside.
LEE: The gas man would run out from his warm office and
   pump our gas without bothering with a coat. Waitresses
   would lift me light as a feather over someone's head
   and plop me down in the back of a booth. Everyone
   seemed so strong to me then.
BESSIE: We were little.
LEE: Seemed like such a long trip.
BESSIE: Forever.

(MARVIN *stirs again.* BESSIE *and* LEE *are quiet for a moment.*)

Are you seeing anybody now?
LEE: Usually.
BESSIE: I hope you have someone real in your life.
LEE: I don't have much trouble with that.
BESSIE: I'm not talking about "that."
LEE: You should be. There's no reason you haven't had love in your life.
BESSIE: I think I've—
LEE: Men. There's no reason. You're not ugly, Bessie.
BESSIE: Thank you.
LEE: You're not. I know lots of boys were interested in you—they just thought you were stuck-up.
BESSIE: Thank you.
LEE: Well, if you had given them any encouragement . . .
BESSIE: I had a true love.
LEE: You did?
BESSIE: Yes.
LEE: Did he know?
BESSIE: Yes.
LEE: You mean you had a boyfriend?
BESSIE: Yes, I had a boyfriend. Why is that such news?
LEE: How could I not have known about it?
BESSIE: It wasn't anyone you knew.
LEE: Bart Martick.
BESSIE: No. Why do you say Bart Martick?
LEE: I remember you used to stare at him out of the side of your face.
BESSIE: No, I don't remember that. Well, maybe I *would* stare at him, because he had that lazy eye, but it was never anything romantic.
LEE: Who then?

BESSIE: You don't know him.

LEE: You can tell me, Bessie. It's not like I'm going to tell anybody.

BESSIE: Clarence James.

LEE: Who?

BESSIE: I told you you didn't know him.

LEE: How could I not know him?

BESSIE: He was only around in the summers.

(Pause.)

LEE *(catching on)*: You went with a carny worker.

BESSIE: He was a very nice person.

LEE: I didn't say anything.

BESSIE: This is why I kept it a secret.

LEE: I didn't say anything. Daddy would have killed you.

BESSIE: Well, he's never going to know.

LEE: There were some cute ones.

BESSIE: He was cute.

LEE: Which one was he?

BESSIE: He mostly ran the ferris wheel.

LEE: Uh-huh.

BESSIE: I knew he liked me because he always gave me an extra turn.

LEE: That's sweet.

BESSIE: Once he kept my car swaying at the top until I started to cry.

LEE: He was a flirt.

BESSIE: He had these big ears.

LEE: I remember him. He was cute.

BESSIE: He always said he probably came from England because of his name. Clarence James. He'd make a big deal out of his manners. He had the funniest laugh.

He'd open his mouth real wide and no sound would come out.

LEE: He was only there about three summers.

BESSIE: Four summers.

LEE: Then he stopped coming.

BESSIE: That's right.

(Pause.)

LEE: What happened?

BESSIE: Nothing like you think.

LEE: What happened?

BESSIE: They always have a last picnic down by the river. This year there was kind of a cold snap, so a lot of people were bundled up. But Clarence—he'll deny it, but he likes to be the center of attention. Clarence goes swimming anyway. And he knows everybody is watching him. Everybody is there—his family, his friends, me. And he bobs up out of the water and he's laughing, making that monkey face, which gets all of us laughing, and he dunks under again and pops up somewhere else laughing even harder, which gets *us* laughing even harder. And he dives under again and then he doesn't come up and doesn't come up and he doesn't come up. Laughing and choking looked the same on Clarence. He drowned right in front of us. Every time he came up for air, there we were chuckling and pointing. What could he have thought?

LEE: Bessie, you should have told me.

BESSIE: If I couldn't tell people I had a carny boyfriend, I couldn't tell people my carny boyfriend drowned.

LEE: You should have told me anyway.

BESSIE: We were never that close.

LEE: Weren't we?

BESSIE: No.

(Pause.)

LEE: Do you want me to do something with that wig?
BESSIE: What?
LEE: I don't know. Let me look at it.

(BESSIE turns her head, giving LEE a look.)

  No, you have to take it off.
BESSIE: Oh.
LEE: I won't hurt it.

(BESSIE is reluctant to give LEE the wig.)

  This is a nice wig, Bessie. It's nicely ventilated. We can
  do something with this. Do you want me to?
BESSIE: Sure.

*(BESSIE takes off her wig and hands it to LEE. A long
pause as LEE takes in the effects of Bessie's chemotherapy.)*

LEE: I'm glad we made this trip. I only wish we could stay
  longer. This is a nice weave.

(RUTH enters.)

RUTH: Bessie? Bessie?
BESSIE: Ruth? *(She ties a scarf over her head.)*
RUTH: I went by your room. You weren't there.
BESSIE: I'm here.
RUTH: It was empty.
BESSIE: I'm here.

(RUTH *hugs* BESSIE *hard.*)

BESSIE: Oh, honey, I'm still here. Honeybunch.

(LEE *turns away, brushing out the wig with her fingers.*)

(*Blackout.*)

SCENE FOUR

(Walt Disney World. HANK sits alone on a bench. LEE enters with two Cokes. She gives one to HANK and joins him on the bench. They drink.)

LEE: These are expensive.
HANK: This is the Diet.
LEE: Is it?

(They switch drinks. They drink.)

That Swiss Family Robinson tree house is huge.

HANK: I guess.
LEE: We saw that movie. Do you remember? I took you. I took you both. That's when I was still driving the Plymouth. Do you remember?
HANK: I don't remember.
LEE: I took you both to that movie.
HANK: I remember Dad took us to *The Planet of the Apes.*
LEE: No, he didn't.

HANK: He didn't?

LEE: I took you to that, but you were older then.

(Pause.)

HANK: That was a good movie.

LEE: The one with the apes?

HANK: Uh-huh.

LEE: Oh, good. I'm glad you liked it. Are you having a good time?

HANK: Where's Charlie?

LEE: They're probably still at the Hall of Presidents. You didn't want to see that. . . . I'm proud of you, Hank, getting tested for Bessie.

HANK: Are we going to sit here all day?

LEE: We're supposed to meet them here. Maybe we'll eat. Or we'll see that movie that wraps around you.

HANK: Charlie and I want to go to Space Mountain.

LEE: We'll do that.

HANK: We want to go off by ourselves.

LEE: No. Uh-uh. I've already gone back on my ultimatum just letting you come. I think you're doing really well this trip. I think everyone is going to hear how well you did. I think it will mean a lot to them. For the most part your behavior down here has made me very happy. But no. *(Pause.)* That submarine ride. Now, that's a movie too.

HANK: Did we see that one?

LEE: Did you? *(She tries hard to remember.)* I don't think so. I don't remember.

HANK: With Dad?

LEE: No, no, no, not with your dad. Do you like apes? Do you like animals?

(HANK stands and hurls his Coke offstage. He sits.)

Hank! You're not getting another one. *(Pause.)* Do you want to know something about your dad? On Saturday I worked and your dad took care of you.

HANK: He did?

LEE: Yeah. And sometimes on Saturdays you'd get hurt. And I know you roughhoused too much. And I'd yell at you for roughhousing too much, but you'd still get hurt. And I started leaving my job early so I could get home and . . . I'd yell at you and yell at you and beg you to please stop hurting yourself, because he was my husband, and I loved him, and what was I supposed to do? Then Charlie came, and I just . . . *(Pause.)* My feelings for you, Hank, are like a big bowl of fish hooks. I can't just pick them up one at a time. I pick up one, they all come. So I tend to leave them alone.

(CHARLIE pushes RUTH on in a wheelchair. CHARLIE is wearing a Goofy cap and RUTH, a sun hat.)

RUTH: Oh! There you are. It's like a piece of heaven fell from the sky. Isn't it? So many handsome young men and women. Everyone is so nice. Mickey Mouse pushed my chair for a little while. Didn't he, Charlie?

CHARLIE: He did.

LEE: Is he still around? I want to get a picture.

RUTH: I don't know where he went. He's probably very busy.

LEE: Where's Bessie?

RUTH: She's getting Cokes for everyone.

LEE: She is?

RUTH: You should have come with us. You don't know what you missed.

LEE: Did you like the Hall of Presidents?

RUTH: It was so nice to see FDR again.

LEE: Are you hungry, Charlie?

CHARLIE *(who has started to read a book)*: Not yet.

LEE: Charlie, please don't read. You're at Disney World. Look around.

RUTH: Do you want me to hold your book on my lap?

CHARLIE: No.

LEE: Read your book if you want. It doesn't matter.

(BESSIE enters with a tray of Cokes. Her wig has been styled; it looks very nice.)

BESSIE: Here we are. I hope everyone is thirsty. Hank. *(She gives him a Coke.)* Lee.

LEE: I already have one.

BESSIE: We have an extra, then. Hank, you look extra thirsty. *(She gives him a second Coke.)* Ruth.

RUTH: It looks nice and cold.

BESSIE: Charlie. Isn't it a beautiful day? I feel like I haven't been outside in years.

LEE: Did you like the Hall of Presidents?

BESSIE: It was kind of fun to see JFK again.

RUTH *(starts waving frantically)*: Lee, there's one of those cartoon characters if you want to get a picture.

LEE: Who is that? Pluto?

RUTH: It looks more like a gopher than a dog.

BESSIE: Those aren't gopher ears.

LEE: Is Pluto a dog?

CHARLIE *(looking up from his book)*: Yes.

BESSIE: They look like horse ears.

LEE: Let's get our picture taken with it.

HANK: I don't want my picture taken with some mutant.

BESSIE: Should we wait for someone more Disney?

RUTH: Like Daisy Duck?

LEE: C'mon, Hank.

BESSIE: This you can probably see at Six Flags.

LEE: But we're all together now. I'm going to ask him to come over.

(She exits.)

HANK: Charlie, let's go to Space Mountain.
CHARLIE: Okay.
BESSIE: I don't think your mom wants you to go off alone.
HANK: She doesn't care.
BESSIE: I think she does.
HANK: We'll be right back.
BESSIE: Hank, stay here.
HANK: We'll only be gone a second.
BESSIE: Hank, please.
HANK: Okay.

(LEE re-enters.)

LEE: That was the rudest cartoon character I've ever met. He knew damn well what I was asking him, but he just kept bobbing his head and waving his hooves at me like some dumb animal.
RUTH: Hooves?
LEE: Hooves, paws. Was I supposed to tip him?
CHARLIE: No.
LEE: Well, we'll just have to get someone else. What did you want to do next, Ruth? See It's a Small World?
RUTH: If everyone else does.
LEE: Sure, why don't we?
BESSIE: You all go ahead. I want to sit here a bit.
LEE: We can sit longer.
BESSIE: No. I'm fine. I just want to sit in the sun. I'll catch up to you.
LEE: Where?
HANK: How about Space Mountain?

BESSIE: Space Mountain in an hour?

LEE: Okay.

RUTH: Why don't you come, Bessie?

BESSIE: It feels good to sit in the sun. And if I come somebody will have to ride by themselves.

LEE: We'll see you in front of Space Mountain in an hour. Right where the line starts.

BESSIE: I'll be there.

LEE: Charlie, do you want me to push your aunt for a while?

CHARLIE: I like pushing.

RUTH: You're a good driver.

(They are off.)

(BESSIE shuts her eyes and breathes deeply. She is not feeling well. The feeling passes. She sips her Coke from a straw. It comes away bloody. She puts her finger in her mouth. More blood. She stares at it. She puts her hand to her mouth. There is blood in her mouth. It gets on her hand. She stands as if to go. A cartoon character enters as BESSIE faints and falls to the ground. The cartoon character turns and walks toward the audience waving as the lights fade.)

SCENE FIVE

(*Walt Disney World: the Lost Children's hut.* BESSIE *lies on a small bed.* LEE *sits in a small chair.*)

(BESSIE *wakes up violently as if from a nightmare.*)

LEE: You're all right.
BESSIE: Hmmmm.
LEE: You're all right.
BESSIE: Where am I?
LEE: You're in the Lost Children's hut.
BESSIE: Where?

(RUTH *appears in the doorway.*)

RUTH: Bessie?
LEE: She's okay, Ruth.
BESSIE: Ruth?
RUTH: Bessie?
BESSIE: I'm fine.
RUTH: Are you all right now?

BESSIE: I just got real tired.

RUTH: You should rest.

BESSIE: I am.

RUTH: You do too much. You always do too much.

BESSIE: I won't do so much anymore. I promise.

LEE: She's fine, Ruth.

BESSIE: We've only paid Dad's nurse till seven o'clock.

LEE: Don't worry about that.

BESSIE: Is there a phone?

RUTH: I'll call.

(She exits.)

LEE: Dr. Serat and Dr. Wally are meeting us at the
    hospital.

BESSIE: Dr. Serat?

LEE: He's back.

BESSIE: I have to go back in the hospital?

LEE: They want to look at you. If you feel good there's
    no reason you can't come home.

BESSIE: I feel good.

LEE: What happened?

BESSIE: I fainted.

LEE: From the heat?

BESSIE: There was blood in my mouth.

LEE: Is your mouth still bleeding?

BESSIE: No. Did a doctor look at me?

LEE: No. He just thought you fainted so he carried you in
    here to lie down.

BESSIE: Who's "he"?

LEE: The gopher man.

BESSIE: The gopher man?

LEE: Yes.

BESSIE: Carried me to the Lost Children's hut?

LEE: He just thought you fainted. He didn't know you had been bleeding.

BESSIE: I couldn't have bled that much.

LEE: Maybe you were kind of faint from not eating, too. That might be all it is.

BESSIE: I fainted because . . . I was scared.

LEE: You're all right.

BESSIE: I was so scared.

LEE: That's okay.

BESSIE: What's happening to me?

LEE: Sssh.

BESSIE: I can't sleep. I never sleep. I'm afraid to close my eyes . . . I'll close my eyes and I won't wake up. So I jerk myself awake. I yank myself awake all night long.

LEE: Bessie . . .

BESSIE: I pour myself some coffee.

LEE: It's okay.

BESSIE: I just want to find a place to hide.

LEE: You're okay.

BESSIE: I'm trying to be brave.

LEE: Shh. Shh.

BESSIE: But I'm scared. I'm so scared.

(They hug.)

LEE: Ssh. Ssh. You're okay. Oh, you're okay. *(She comforts BESSIE silently.)* What have you got to be scared of? Everything is going to be okay. You'll see. There's still Hank and Charlie. Are you forgetting that? You're okay.

BESSIE: Where are they?

LEE: They're sitting out front.

BESSIE: Was Space Mountain fun?

LEE: Uh-huh. It was real fun.

BESSIE: You're lucky to have those boys.

LEE: I know I am.

BESSIE: They're good boys, both of them.

LEE: Yes, they are.

BESSIE: And you know?

LEE: What?

BESSIE: I'm lucky to have Dad and Ruth.

LEE: Mm-hmm.

BESSIE: I've had such love in my life. I look back and I've had such love.

LEE: They love you very much.

BESSIE: I don't mean . . . I mean *I* love *them*. I am so lucky to have been able to love someone so much. I am so lucky to have loved so much. I am so lucky.

LEE: Yes, you are. You are.

BESSIE: We're fooling ourselves, Lee.

(HANK *appears in the doorway.*)

LEE: How?

BESSIE: Hank and Charlie aren't going to match.

LEE: We don't know that.

BESSIE: They're my nephews. They're once removed.

LEE: It could still happen.

BESSIE: I don't want to pretend any longer. We have too many decisions to make before you leave.

LEE: We don't have to make them right now.

HANK: Is that true?

LEE (*noticing* HANK): Hank, would you find me a wheelchair?

HANK: Charlie is.

LEE (*to* BESSIE): Do you feel up to going to the car?

BESSIE: Oh, sure.

(BESSIE *sits up.* CHARLIE *enters with a wheelchair and stops it next to the tiny chair.* HANK *picks* BESSIE *up and puts her in the wheelchair. She looks at the tiny chair.*)

BESSIE: I don't remember ever being that small.
LEE: Ready?

(*Blackout.*)

SCENE SIX

(Night. HANK *and* CHARLIE *in their sleeping bags.)*

HANK: Charlie? Charlie?

(Pause. HANK *goes to* CHARLIE, *straddles him, and shines a pen light in his face.)* Charlie?

CHARLIE: What?
HANK: What are you doing?
CHARLIE: Sleeping. What are you doing?
HANK: Can't sleep.
CHARLIE: How come?
HANK: How come you do so bad in school?
CHARLIE: I don't know.
HANK: You gotta study more.
CHARLIE: Get off me.
HANK: This is cool. Your eyes shrink when I shine the light on them.
CHARLIE: I can't breathe.

HANK: And quit letting Mom buy all your clothes. You
   look like a geek.

CHARLIE: You're going to make me blind.

HANK: And pay more attention. Okay?

CHARLIE: Okay.

(HANK sits back down. Pause.)

I don't think I look so bad.

HANK: Did you hear what I said?

CHARLIE: Yeah.

HANK: Okay. Charlie, how much money you got down
   here?

CHARLIE: I have fifteen dollars and thirty-six cents left.

HANK: Why'd you buy that stupid Goofy cap?

CHARLIE: I like it.

HANK: If I ever take anything from you, you know I'll
   find a way to pay you back.

(Pause.)

CHARLIE: Hank?

HANK: Go to sleep now.

(Blackout.)

SCENE SEVEN

(Bessie's home. RUTH *sits in her chair.* CHARLIE *stands over her. Lee's makeup kit is open and spread on* RUTH's *lap.* RUTH *is dressed up.)*

RUTH *(handing* CHARLIE *an eyeliner)*: Try this one.
CHARLIE: I'm afraid I'll poke you in the eye.
RUTH: Oh, no. I trust you. You've got a steady hand. Not like me.
CHARLIE: Look up. *(He applies the eyeliner.)*
RUTH: Not too heavy.
CHARLIE: Okay.
RUTH: I don't mean to tell you what to do.
CHARLIE: No, tell me.
RUTH: I haven't had reason to pretty myself up since—I can't think when.
CHARLIE: Today's the day.
RUTH: I hope nothing goes wrong. They almost got married once before, but the church caught fire.
CHARLIE: Is Coral the same character who shot Lance's dad in the head?

RUTH: Mm-hmm.

CHARLIE: And now they're getting married?

RUTH: Well, he lived. And she felt awful about it.

CHARLIE: How's that?

RUTH: Oh, what a good job!

CHARLIE: You look pretty.

RUTH: I do not. If I look anything at all it's because you're such a help. Charlie, where's Hank? I want him to move the TV from my room into Bessie's room so she can watch too.

CHARLIE: I can do it.

RUTH: Are you sure?

CHARLIE: Yeah.

(As CHARLIE *exits:)*

RUTH: It's awfully heavy.

(LEE enters.)

LEE: Let me see, Ruth. Oh, you're beautiful.

RUTH: Don't make fun of me.

LEE: I'm not.

RUTH: I'm a silly old woman dressing up for a TV show.

LEE: You're not. I'm going to make some snacks so we won't be getting up during the program.

RUTH: Oh, my. It's becoming such a production. Is everybody going to watch?

LEE: I don't know if Hank is. I don't know where he's got to.

RUTH: I'll find him.

LEE: It's so nice to have you up and around, Ruth. It must be wonderful to be rid of constant pain.

RUTH: Oh, yes. Though I do sometimes miss it.

(She exits.)

(LEE puts chips into a bowl. CHARLIE re-enters, reading his book. He takes some chips, crosses to a chair and begins to read.)

(BESSIE enters.)

LEE: What are you doing up?

BESSIE: I'm going to give Dad his one o'clock.

LEE: I was going to do that.

BESSIE: Oh, I can do it.

LEE: You're supposed to be taking it easy.

BESSIE: I am.

LEE: Do you want something to snack on?

BESSIE: Better just cut me up some fruit.

(The phone rings.)

LEE *(answering)*: Hello? . . . Hello, Dr. Serat.

BESSIE: What is it?

LEE: It's Dr. Serat. He wants to talk to you.

BESSIE: Hello. . . . Oh, you did. Good. . . . Um . . . uh . . . what is—. . . I see. . . . I see. . . . Uh-huh. Then should I keep taking what I'm taking now? . . . No, I understand. . . . I'm not. Thank you, doctor. Goodbye. *(She hangs up.)* They got Hank and Charlie's test results back and it looks like it didn't work out.

LEE: Oh, Bessie.

BESSIE: That's pretty much what we expected. We knew the odds were against it.

LEE: Maybe we should do them again. Maybe they made a mistake.

BESSIE: Maybe, but I don't . . . I'm supposed to continue

with the therapies I'm doing now and see what kind of
luck I have.

LEE: That's right. Those are good things to be doing.

BESSIE: Where's Hank? We should tell Hank. I was in the
middle of doing something. What was I . . . ? Oh, Dad.
*(She reaches for the pills and knocks them onto the floor.
The pills spill all over.)*

LEE: Do you want to go lie down?

BESSIE: No. I'm fine, I just . . . *(She starts picking up the
pills.)*

LEE: I can do that. Charlie.

(CHARLIE and LEE help pick up the pills.)

BESSIE: It's what we thought. It's not a surprise. It's what
I always had in the back of my head. Now I don't have
to think about it anymore. I can quit thinking about it.
(Sigh of relief.) Oh, I can quit thinking about it. We
should tell Hank.

LEE: Charlie, where's your brother?

CHARLIE: He's gotta be somewhere.

LEE *(calling):* Hank?

(She exits.)

CHARLIE: Hank ran away.

BESSIE: What?

CHARLIE: He ran away last night.

BESSIE: Oh, Charlie, no.

CHARLIE: He left you this.

(He hands BESSIE a note. She reads it to herself.)

CHARLIE: I didn't read it.

BESSIE *(reading the note to CHARLIE)*: "Aunt Bessie, gone

someplace else. Goodbye, good luck. I love you, too. Hank."

CHARLIE: He said he was sorry he couldn't wait.

(They hug.)

BESSIE: Oh, Charlie. We have to tell your mother.

CHARLIE: I promised I wouldn't tell until tonight.

BESSIE: Charlie, she has to know.

CHARLIE: Aunt Bessie, I promised. It was the last thing I said.

BESSIE: Do you want me to tell her?

CHARLIE: I promised.

BESSIE: Why don't you go on outside?

(CHARLIE exits. BESSIE reads the note again. She is overcome and is beginning to break down when MARVIN stirs in his room.)

BESSIE: Dad? What is it? What's wrong? It's just me. There's nothing to be afraid of.

(MARVIN calms down.)

There's nothing to be afraid of.

(She leaves the note on the counter and goes into Marvin's room.)

(LEE enters and sees some pills still on the floor. She picks up the pills and pill bottle from the floor and crosses to the counter to put them down. She sees Hank's note and reads it to herself. After a few moments she crumbles the note, tosses it on the counter, and begins to exit.

(Before she can leave, HANK enters with his bags. He does not see LEE. He crosses to the chair, drops his bags, goes to look into Marvin's room, stops, turns back

to the chair, and sees LEE. *The two look at each other from across the room.* HANK *removes his bandanna.)*

RUTH *(offstage):* Hurry up, Charlie. The show's starting.

(HANK crosses past LEE and exits. LEE *crosses to the chair and picks up Hank's bags.)*

BESSIE *(in Marvin's room):* Here, let me do this for you.

(BESSIE starts bouncing the light around Marvin's room. LEE *exits. The lights fade down to* BESSIE *and* MARVIN. *Then the lights get very bright in Marvin's room. After a moment, they fade back down to* BESSIE *and* MARVIN, *who are heard laughing. Then the lights fade completely out.)*